complete
origami

complete
origami

EASY TECHNIQUES
25 GREAT PROJECTS

DAVID MITCHELL

FIREFLY BOOKS

A FIREFLY BOOK

Published by Firefly Books Ltd. 2009

Publisher Cataloging-in-Publication Data (U.S.)

Mitchell, David, 1952-
    Complete origami : easy techniques and 25 great
projects / David Mitchell.
[160] p. : col. photos.; cm.
Summary: Projects ranging from beginner to
advance.
ISBN-13: 978-1-55407-459-4 (pbk.)
ISBN-10: 1-55407-459-2 (pbk.)
1. Origami. I. Title.
736/.982 dc22   TT870.M583 2009

Library and Archives Canada Cataloguing in
Publication

Mitchell, David, 1952-
    Complete origami : easy techniques and 25
great projects / David Mitchell.
ISBN-13: 978-1-55407-459-4
ISBN-10: 1-55407-459-2
    1. Origami. I. Title.
TT870.M468 2009   736'.982   C2008-906057-1

Published in the United States by
Firefly Books (U.S.) Inc.
P.O. Box 1338, Ellicott Station
Buffalo, New York 14205

Published in Canada by
Firefly Books Ltd.
66 Leek Crescent
Richmond Hill, Ontario L4B 1H1

Cover design by Jacqueline Hope Raynor

Printed in China

The publisher gratefully acknowledges the financial
support for our publishing program by the
Government of Canada through the Book Publishing
Industry Development Program.

contents

6   introduction
8   history of origami
14 before you begin
22 folding symbols

projects

24 **kabuto** - pure origami
28 **banana boat** - using irogami
32 **cormorant on a rock** - introducing reverse folds
38 **juxtaposition** - starting from standard grids
44 **piranha** - developing traditional bases
50 **tsuru** - the bird base
56 **clingons** - combining finished designs
60 **lover's knot** - the pull-out squash
66 **chinese goldfish** - inflatable areas

70 **fish bowl** - simple transformations
76 **flapping parrot** - beyond standard bases
82 **tato** - altering the angles
88 **give me sunshine** - crease and collapse designs
92 **egypt** - changing the starting shape
96 **perfect elephant** - elements of origami design
102 **shipwreck** - combining multiple sheets
108 **coasters** - integrating multiple sheets

114 **artifact** - working with silver rectangles
120 **dresden bowl** - creating curves
126 **lovebird** - using translucency
130 **david's star** - origami tessellations
136 **enigma bowl** - developing complex bases
142 **gaia** - developing complex form
148 **windfarm** - sub-dividing sheets
154 **stargate** - integrating modular assemblies
160 resources

introduction

Origami means folding paper. It's that simple and that complicated, too. Origami began small but has grown big. As recently as the 1970s it was quite possible for an enthusiast to know almost every design in the origami repertoire. Today, that is quite impossible, even in the many specialist fields that have developed within origami. There are just too many designs out there and more are created every day. They multiply, in fact, like origami rabbits.

This book, then, cannot be an exhaustive catalog of origami designs and styles. What it can be is an introduction to the major ideas that underlie origami design and give a broad overview of the most important techniques that are used to realize those ideas in paper. In order to make clear connections between these ideas I have tried to link the projects together. You will find enough origami fish in this book to stock a small aquarium, as well as several birds, elephants, boats and bowls. It is easier to understand the difference between design techniques when they are used to create similar subjects. But you will also find more unusual subjects too, a partly-sunken ship, a landscape, sunshine and many beautiful geometric designs.

I have also tried to strike a balance between designs folded from single sheets and those that use several, or even many. Modular origami is my passion, but I have tried to restrain myself and give other techniques a fair chance, too.

The techniques section of this book tells you all you need to know about how to fold paper and how to read origami diagrams. The individual chapters will introduce you to lots of new ideas about design techniques, origami ethics and creative ideas, but there is one over-arching idea that you need to know

about right now, and that is the idea of elegance. Elegance is a quality that origami designs either have or lack. It isn't something you can understand by looking at the finished design, or by studying the diagrams. Nor is it something you can easily define. Elegance is a tactile quality; more of a feeling than anything else. You have to actually fold the design to understand it. Elegant design sequences flow. Inelegant ones seem to be contrived, or are difficult to fold. Maybe the layers get too thick, or you seem to have to force the paper into shape. You'll know elegance when you find it because the paper almost seems to fold itself. And you will very definitely find it in the designs in this book which have been chosen very much with elegance, rather than, say, efficiency, verisimilitude, or cleverness in mind.

It is not, perhaps, too much to say that it is elegance that sets origami apart from other papercrafts, indeed from other crafts in general. Origami is not so much about the destination as the journey. The result is important, but how you get there is more important still.

Paperfolding, in all its incredible variety, has fascinated me since I was a child. It is remarkable what can be created from ordinary paper, just by folding it — something that almost all of us can easily do. I hope that this book will not only help you to understand what origami is all about, but also to derive as much pleasure and satisfaction from folding paper as I do.

history of origami

The Invention of Paper: Since folding paper is such a natural thing to do, it is likely that paperfolding, in its broadest sense, is almost as old as paper itself. According to Chinese tradition, paper was first invented by T'sai Lun, a senior court official working for the Chinese Emperor Yuan Hsing, in the year 105. T'sai Lun's paper was made from fibers obtained from bark, rags and old fish nets and was intended to be used as a medium for writing on (though the Chinese also used other media, such as flattened bamboo strips, for this purpose). This kind of paper would probably not have folded at all well, and so very early paperfolding was probably only of the kind that can be called 'everyday origami', where paper is folded for purely practical purposes such as concealing the contents of a letter from open view.

The Japanese tradition: According to Japanese tradition, knowledge of how to make paper was first brought to Japan in 610 by the Buddhist monk Dokyo. The plant fibers available to papermakers in Japan soon enabled them to produce strong, crisp papers of exceptionally high quality. Paper of this kind folds well and over the next 1000 years a tradition of craft paperfolding slowly evolved.

At first, much of Japanese paperfolding was ceremonial in nature, largely concerned with the folding of wrappers, known as 'tsutsumi' or 'noshi', which were used to contain and decorate gifts, especially gifts of flowers associated with religious festivals. Folk memories of this practice still survive in the design of some gift wrappings in Japan today.

During the same period, folded paper butterflies began to be used to decorate the sake (Japanese rice wine) containers used in wedding ceremonies and these butterflies may well have been the earliest examples of representational origami designs.

Gradually, the ceremonial type of paperfolding gave rise to a folk tradition of folding paper into simple representational and practical designs, such as the well-known Tsuru (see page 50), Yakkosan (or the man-servant) and the Masu. By 1728, sufficient folds were known to enable them to be collected into the Go-hyaku Oribako or 'Box of 500 Folds.' Unfortunately the folds themselves have not survived so we have no idea which designs were included in the collection.

The Senzaburu Orikata: The year 1797 saw the publication in Japan of two books of origami designs which have survived. The most important of these is called _The Senzaburu Orikata_ or 'Folding 1000 Cranes,' a book of origami designs, woodcuts and poetry. Senzaburu means 1000 cranes, Orikata is an old word for origami. The number 1000 in the title is used symbolically. If you folded all the designs in the book you would only have folded about 250 cranes in all.

It is not clear whether _The Senzaburu Orikata_ is a collection of traditional designs or an explanation of the design work of one particular paperfolder. Perhaps it is both. One of the important techniques it introduces is the sub-dividing of large sheets into smaller sheets by means of slits. This type of paperfolding is sometimes called Rokoan style. The most complex design featured in _The Senzaburu Orikata_ is the 'Hundred Cranes,' though without any accompanying instruction.

The Kayaragusa: Another interesting collection of diagrams for origami designs, _The Kayaragusa_ (also known as the _Kan No Mado_ or 'Window on Midwinter'), was compiled in 1845, though it was not published publicly until 1961. This compilation

contains a much more varied collection of models, including a dragonfly, lobster, octopus, snail and various human figures, and is evidence of the existence of a vibrant paperfolding tradition in which a large variety of creative techniques were in use. Most of the arms and legs for the complex figures are obtained by cutting slits into the starting shape used, but the manuscript also contains instructions for important uncut designs such as the traditional Frog. Many of the designs in *The Kayaragusa* make use of the 'inflatable areas' technique (see page 66) in which a hollow section of the design is inflated to form, for instance, the head or body of the subject.

Surprisingly little is known about the Japanese folk origami tradition after 1845. Perhaps it continued to develop. Perhaps it went into decline. Hard evidence is lacking. We simply do not know when many traditional designs originated or in many cases if they are truly traditional at all.

Other traditions: To the extent that it existed, the Chinese paperfolding tradition was probably also largely ceremonial, mainly concerned with the production of Yuen Bao (gold nuggets) and other items to be burned at funerals. Yuen Bao are characterized by the way in which they are first folded flat and then 'three-dimensionalized' by pulling the center of the design apart. The Chinese Junk (if it is indeed Chinese) shown below is more probably a Yuen Bao of this kind, than a representation of a ship.

Some evidence of a non-ceremonial Chinese tradition does exist. In particular, two notably elegant geometric origami designs, the Lazy Susan and Verdi's Vase are almost certainly of Chinese origin.

Evidence for a tradition of paperfolding in Western Europe is largely based around the folding of baptismal

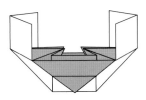

certificates, the work of Friedrich Froebel, and a few simple folds such as the Pajarita (Cocotte), the traditional dart, and the Newspaper Hat (plus the boat into which it can be turned).

Charles Dodgson (Lewis Carrol) mentions such boats, together with paper pistols, several times in his letters. The popular Victorian/Edwardian parlor game known as Consequences also made use of folded paper.

Akira Yoshizawa: On March 14, 1911, Japan's most-gifted model-making paperfolder, Akira Yoshizawa, was born. By the late 1950s, working largely alone, he had revolutionized origami design and folding techniques (in particular by devising ways of creating multiple points without the necessity for using cuts), and created a huge number of new and highly realistic models of animals, insects, fish and birds. His emphasis on naturalistic realism led him to abandon the traditional technique of folding dry paper in favor of the oddly misnamed technique known as 'wet-folding' in which paper is first dampened and then moulded into soft-folds, the shape of which it retains as it dries. Yoshizawa's influence on the development of origami design in the modern era cannot be overestimated.

Origami in the West: The real history of origami in the West begins with the end of Japanese political and cultural isolation in 1945. Up to that time information about Japanese culture had been scarce and difficult to obtain. Now it was freely available for those who cared to look hard enough.

The writer and researcher Gershon Legman (better known for his collections of erotica and rude limericks) was one of those who did. In 1945, while recovering from a broken ankle, he whiled away his time folding origami designs remembered from his childhood. The enthusiasm for paperfolding this wakened in him led him to research the subject in depth. His research eventually led him to discover the work of Akira Yoshizawa and in 1955 he arranged an exhibition of Yoshizawa's designs at the Stedelijk Museum in Amsterdam.

From seeds like this sufficient interest in origami arose in the West, notably in the U.S. and Britain, to enable the formation of origami clubs and organizations such as the Portfolio Society (later to metamorphose into the British Origami Society) and the Origami Center of America (later to become Origami USA). Almost from the very first, the members of these societies were concerned not only to catalog as many traditional designs as possible, but also to create their own original designs and to push the boundaries of what was possible in terms of subject matter and technique.

Since the formation of the Western origami societies, a huge number of original designs have been produced, many of them of admittedly dubious quality but others of sufficient merit to take their place in the design portfolio familiar to many, if not most, members of the international origami community. One intriguing consequence of this proliferation has been the development of origami societies in Japan. Before the growth of interest in the West, paperfolding in Japan was of a relatively lowly cultural status, being enjoyed largely by mothers and their children. Even Akira Yoshizawa had difficulty getting his work published. Western interest, however, has provoked an origami renaissance in Japan, where paperfolding is now seen as an acceptable academic hobby and practiced by many intellectuals and professionals.

Modular origami: Although its roots are now known to go back to at least 1734, modular origami (see page 154) is largely a modern phenomenon. The modular

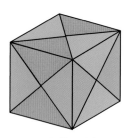

technique was quite independently re-invented, first by Robert Neale in the U.S., and later by Mitsonobu Sonobe (Mitsonobu's Cube, left) in Japan. Since then, many paperfolding designers have expanded the modular repertoire, some of whom have specialized in modular design to the virtual exclusion of any other.

The influence of mathematics: Origami is amenable to detailed mathematical analysis, both in terms of the relationships of different parts of the paper within the sheet (which remain fixed however the sheet is folded — at least in the absence of cuts) and in the spatial relationships between points outside the sheet (which vary as folds are formed). In recent years, model-making paperfolders, particularly in the U.S. and Japan, most notably Robert Lang, have developed mathematical design tools that make it possible to create realistically proportioned designs which also make highly efficient use of the paper (though they may not always be either easy or elegant to fold). Whether, in the long term, this development has a positive or a negative effect on the development of origami design remains to be seen.

before you begin

The projects in this book have been graded into three
levels of complexity: beginner, intermediate and
advanced. Unless you are already an experienced folder,
start simple and work your way up. You will achieve
better results on the complex projects once you've
acquired the necessary skills with practice on the more
straightforward designs. The following section will guide
you through the basic first steps in paperfolding. With
each new project in the book, different papers, folds
and techniques will be introduced, building to give you
a complete understanding of this fascinating craft.

About Paper

It would be easy to write a book this size just about paper alone. It can be thick or thin, crisp or soft, translucent or opaque, plain or decorated, smooth or embossed, foldable or brittle or anything in between. Getting a good result in origami is not only about developing skill at folding but also about choosing the right paper for the design. It is hard to give advice about this. It is clearly best to use a thin paper for complex designs, for instance, but mostly it is a case of learning from experience. Gather as many different papers as you can and see what happens when you fold them. For origami purposes, it is important to be able to distinguish between mono, duo and irogami papers.

Mono paper is the same color and pattern on both surfaces (and usually all the way through as well). Machine-made mono paper usually has a slightly different texture on each surface, but this is usually not significant when folding. Writing and photocopying paper are usually mono.

By contrast, the two surfaces of duo paper can be easily distinguished from each other because they are either decorated with different plain colors or patterns. You can get duo paper by buying it from origami paper suppliers or by collecting paper that has only been printed on one surface. Wrapping paper is another good source.

Irogami, a special kind of duo paper manufactured specifically for folding, is white on one surface and a single plain color or pattern on the other. You can buy packs of irogami in pre-cut squares from specialist origami paper retailers, though they may not know it by that name. Paperfolders often call this kind of paper 'kami,' or simply origami paper.

Each project in this book will tell you which of these three kinds of paper is required.

Folds and Creases

Origami diagrams explain the folding sequence that takes you from the blank sheet(s) of paper to the finished design in a step-by-step manner. Each step in the sequence is numbered from 1 to however many steps are required.

A fold is a change in direction in the surface of the paper. A sheet of paper usually starts out flat but you can bend it to become a fold. If you let the bend go, the paper unfolds itself. This resilience is a useful property of paper which many origami designs make use of.

If the paper is bent completely over and flattened so that the folded edge becomes a straight line, you will turn the fold into a crease. Making a crease destroys the paper's resilience along the line of the crease. It breaks some of the connections between the fibers of which the paper is made and creates a permanent line of weakness through the paper. If a fold is creased then opened out, the line of weakness, the crease, still exists. This ability of paper to remember a crease is also useful in origami design.

There are two ways to fold: "in the air" or "on a surface". Folding in the air means folding with the paper held in your hands. Folding on a surface means folding with the paper laid on a flat, hard, surface like the top of a table or a desk. Most people find it more comfortable to fold in the air but more accurate to fold on a surface.

The origami diagrams in this book are drawn as if the paper is laid against a surface. If you need to pick the paper up to make a fold, the written instructions will state where.

A fold is made by bringing the "location points" together. The best way to make an accurate crease is to begin by flattening the center of the fold then to work outwards towards either end. Flatten the crease softly at first then gradually make if stronger and sharper once you know that it is in the right place. To make a strong, sharp crease, you need to finish by flattening the fold completely using a suitable tool.

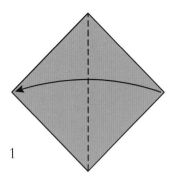

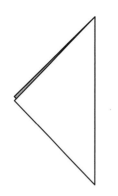

1

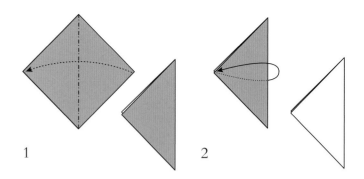

1   2

Moving parts & non-moving parts

If you take a sheet of paper, lay it on a flat surface and fold it in half by laying one edge onto another. You will see that one edge of the paper moves and the other stays still. This is obvious but important. In origami diagrams the fold arrow shows you which part moves and which part stays still. The moving part is the part where the arrow starts and the non-moving part is the part where the arrow ends up.

This is what a diagram for a simple corner-to-corner fold would look like. You will notice that in addition to the fold arrow there is a dashed crease line which shows where the crease will form when the fold is flattened. Below the picture is a written instruction that explains the same thing in words.

1. Fold in half sideways

Location points

The result of following the fold-in-half-sideways instruction is shown above.

In the first picture, the arrow starts near the right-hand corner and ends near the left-hand corner. These two points are the location points for this fold. To make the fold you turn the right-hand corner over, lay it exactly on the left-hand corner, hold it firmly in place then flatten the crease.

Location points can be corners, edges, creases you have already made, or points where creases and edges, or more than one crease, intersect.

Mountains, valleys & hinges

Folds can be made through the paper in two different directions. The edge-to-edge fold shown in the illustration at the far left of this page was made so that the moving part of the paper was folded in front of the non-moving part. We could, however, also make this fold so that the moving part of the paper was folded behind the non-moving part. See diagram 1 above. You will notice that you have to pick the paper up to do this.

Compare the results of making the two folds. If you were using mono paper they would look identical. If you were using duo or irogami, however, the results would be very different (as in diagram 2). These two kinds of folds are called mountain and valley folds.

You can turn a valley into a mountain, and vice versa, just by turning your paper over. You can also turn a mountain fold into a valley fold by reversing the direction of the crease.

You will often come across folds that are made in one direction but which are then reversed at a later stage of the folding sequence. The fact that creases can be reversed means that they can also be used as hinges around which the moving part of the paper can rotate through almost 360°. You can create a hinge by folding the paper forward and backward repeatedly along the crease until it moves easily in both directions. This makes it possible to create designs that incorporate movement.

Instructions for the diagrams above:

1. Pick the paper up then fold in half sideways behind
2. Rotate the rear flap to the front

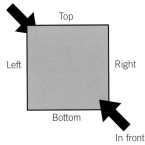

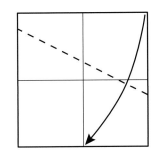

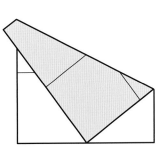

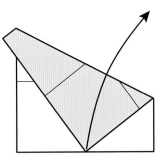

The origami compass

Written instructions use direction words like top, bottom, front and back in the way shown here.

You particularly need to understand the difference between top and front, and bottom and behind, otherwise you will find some of the written instructions confusing.

Before pictures

Each picture in the folding sequence (except the last) is a before picture that shows you how the next fold should be made. A typical before picture (Step 4 of Give Me Sunshine) might look like this and carry the instruction:

4. Fold the top right-hand corner onto the center of the bottom edge.

The picture shows the design at a particular stage in its development. The edges of the paper are shown by thick lines. Creases that have already been made are shown by thin ones. The picture is overlaid with folding symbols that show how the next fold is to be made.

After pictures

Each picture in the folding sequence (apart from the first) is also an after picture which shows the result of making the fold or carrying out the maneuver explained in the previous picture. Here is the after picture for the fold shown to the left.

Combination pictures

Most pictures in the folding sequence will be both before and after pictures, they will show the result of making the previous fold and the instructions for making the next. This can be confusing at times. Just remember to use the picture to check you have made the previous fold correctly before trying to work out what the next fold should be. To illustrate this point, here is the full version of picture 5 above as it appears in the folding instructions for Give Me Sunshine.

5. Crease firmly, then open out the fold made in step 4.

Maneuvers

Maneuvers are actions carried out on the paper which do not create new folds or creases. The simplest kind of maneuver is just turning the paper over sideways, or rotating it through 90° to align with the next picture, but there are more complex maneuvers which involve collapsing the paper into new shapes by using a combination of existing creases, or in which parts of the design are inflated or pulled apart. Like folds, maneuvers are carefully explained both in pictorial and written instructions.

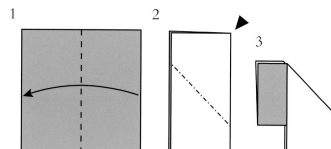

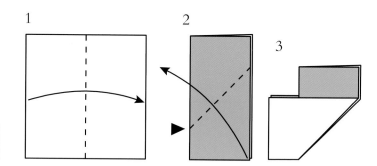

Inside reverse fold

Reverse folds are one of the basic tools in the origami designer's toolkit. They are especially useful if you are trying to design animals or birds. A reverse fold can only be made in a part of the paper that is at least two layers of paper thick and which has one open edge. Reverse folds come in two varieties. They are called inside and outside reverse folds. You will come across them in the third project in the book, Cormorant on a Rock.

In an inside reverse fold the moving parts of the paper are folded in between the layers of the rest of the paper, as shown above with the accompanying instructions:
1. *Fold in half sideways.*
2. *Fold the top right hand point downwards in between the layers.*
3. *This is the result.*

Outside reverse fold

In an outside reverse fold the layers of the moving parts of the paper are separated and are folded outside the rest of the paper, like this:
1. *Fold in half sideways.*
2. *Fold the bottom right-hand point upwards outside the layers.*
3. *This is the result.*
You will notice that in this case the result of following these two folding sequences, using inside and outside reverse folds respectively, is identical. In a simple example like this, either kind of fold can be used. However, when things get a little more complicated, it is quite important to understand the difference between them and how to make both varieties.

Pre-creasing reverse folds

You will notice that when you make a reverse fold, one of the folds in one of the layers is always folded away from you rather than toward you. In the case of an inside reverse fold this is the fold in the front layer. In the case of an outside reverse fold it is the fold in the back layer. Reverse folds are easier to make accurately at first if the folds are pre-creased as simple valley folds. The direction of the crease made in one of the layers of the paper will then need to be reversed (which means it will have to convert a valley fold to a mountain fold or vice versa). This double use of the word reverse in reverse folds and reversing creases is confusing, but it is established origami terminology.

As you get better at folding you will eventually find you can make both kinds of reverse folds accurately without needing to pre-crease the folds.

the folding symbols

These pages contain a short explanation of all the folding symbols you will meet in the course of this book, but you don't need to learn them all now. Just come back to this section as your point of reference. It's time to start folding. The Kabuto awaits…

Edges which lie exactly on top of each other as the result of a fold are normally shown slightly offset on the after diagram.

The edges of the paper are shown as solid lines.

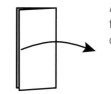

A movement arrow without a fold-line means unfold in the direction indicated.

A folding instruction consists of a movement arrow and a fold-line.

Creases you have already made are shown as thin lines.

A movement arrow shows the direction in which the fold is made.

This version of the fold arrow means fold, crease, then unfold.

The fold-line shows where the new crease will form. A dashed fold-line means that the fold is made towards you.

A dashed and dotted fold-line means that the fold should be made away from you.

Where appropriate, shading is used to distinguish one side of the paper from the other.

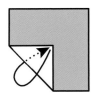

Dotted lines are used to show hidden edges or fold-lines and imaginary lines that are used to help locate a fold.

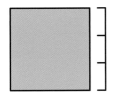

Dotted lines are also used to show the shafts of fold arrows where they pass behind one or more layers of paper. This tells you to swivel the flap to the back by reversing the direction of the existing crease.

This symbol shows that the adjacent edge should be seen as divided into a number of equal sections to help you locate a fold.

This combination of symbols shows you how a combination of existing creases can be used to collapse the paper into a different shape.

This symbol tells you to apply gentle pressure to the paper in the direction the arrowhead is pointing.

This symbol tells you to move the paper gently in the direction of the arrow.

This symbol tells you to turn the paper over.

The rotate symbol tells you to rotate the paper through the number of degrees shown inside the circle before continuing.

This symbol indicates that the next diagram has been drawn on a larger scale.

The eye symbol indicates that the next diagram has been drawn from a different viewpoint.

R

The repeat symbol indicates that a fold has to be repeated on another part of the paper. Refer to the written instruction for details.

○

A circle is used to draw attention to some particular part of a picture referred to in a written explanation or to which you need to pay particular attention when locating a fold.

beginner

★

kabuto

Unlike almost every other craft, origami is about ethics at least as much as it is about aesthetics. In origami, ethics means the rules that paperfolding designers impose upon themselves about what they may, and may not, do in creating and realizing a design. There are many origami ethics but the most important is the idea of pure origami, which basically means that the designs should be achieved simply by folding paper. In pure origami, paper and folding together are enough. The Kabuto is a representation of a traditional Samurai warrior's helmet that completely encapsulates this ideal.

design: traditional japanese

Location Creases

Often the location points for a fold will be part of the existing structure of the design, corners and edges, for instance. Sometimes, however, the location points for a fold have to be created by making extra creases which are not necessary for the design itself. The folds made in Step 4 of the Kabuto, for instance, are only there so that the folds made in step 6 can be made accurately.

The Sideways Squash

The Kabuto also uses a technique called the 'sideways squash.' You will meet this in Steps 14 and 18. In essence this entails picking the design up, separating the layers at the bottom of the design and squashing it flat sideways, so that the two outside corners of the design are brought together in the center. If you have ever folded a newspaper hat and changed it into a boat, you will be familiar with this move.

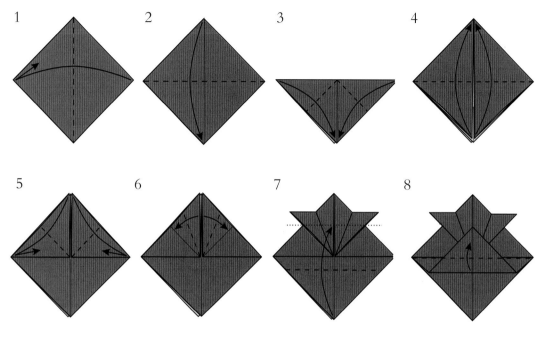

1

2

3

4

5

6

7

8

Materials

Kabuto is created from a square using the simplest of folds, which can all be made individually in isolation from each other. The design works well in ordinary mono paper and almost any weight or size of paper. The Kabuto is therefore a very good place to begin. Both surfaces of the paper are visible on the outside of the finished design.

1 Fold in half sideways, crease, then unfold.

2 Fold in half downward to form a triangle.

3 Fold both outside corners to the bottom.

4 Fold both front flaps in half upward.

5 Fold both front flaps in half outward, crease, then unfold. These creases are used to locate the folds to be made in Step 6.

6 Fold both front flaps outwards as shown.

7 There are two layers at the bottom. Fold the front layer upward as shown.

8 Fold the front layer upward again.

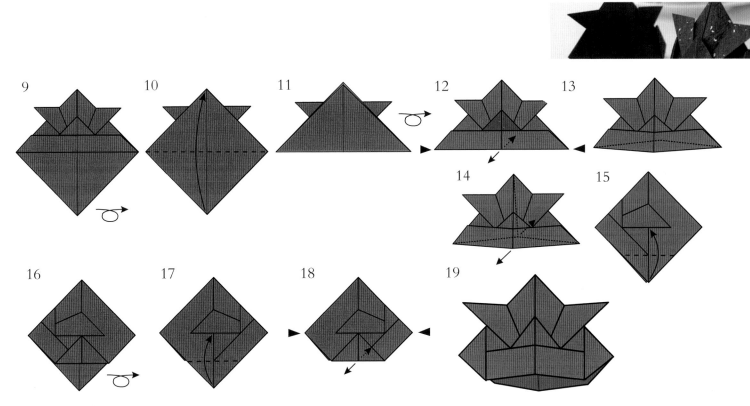

9   Turn the piece over.

10   Fold the bottom point upward.

11   Turn the piece over.

12   Squeeze the model so that the center opens up in front and behind.

13   This is the simplest version of the Kabuto. Steps 14 through 19 show you how to improve it.

14   Squeeze the left- and right-hand corners together until they meet in the center. The result should look like Picture 15.

15   Fold the point of the front layers upwards as shown.

16   Turn the piece over.

17   Repeat Fold 15 on this side of the design.

18   Squeeze the left and right-hand corners together so that the center opens up in front and behind. Continue squeezing until the corners meet in the center.

19   The improved Kabuto is finished.

beginner

★

banana boat

Irogami is paper which is white on one side and a solid color on the other. The contrast between the white and colored surfaces can be used to create patterned shapes or simple paper sketches. In general, paperfolders eschew the use of special effects paper since it is considered a breach of the pure origami ethic, but the use of irogami raises the possibility of manipulating color changes in interesting ways.

Banana Boat is a minimalist paper sketch of a cruise ship or ocean liner in which the colored side of the irogami is used to suggest the hull, and the white side the superstructure. Banana Boat only uses the very simplest kinds of folds, all of which can be made toward you while the paper is lying on a flat surface.

design: david mitchell

Using Irogami

Paperfolding designers may approach the challenge of modeling a subject in different ways. Some aim for anatomical correctness. If an insect has twenty-three appendages they must all be modeled, and if possible, be in the correct proportion to each other. This approach, of course, leads to complexity. Other designers simply aim to achieve a recognizable result, modeling sufficient features that a sheep, for instance, is recognizably a sheep and not just a white guinea pig. A third option is minimalist design, where the designer seeks to produce a recognizable model of a subject in the absolute minimum number of folds. Irogami is very useful in this context. It is much easier to produce minimalist designs when the contrast between colored and white areas can be used to assist the recognition process.

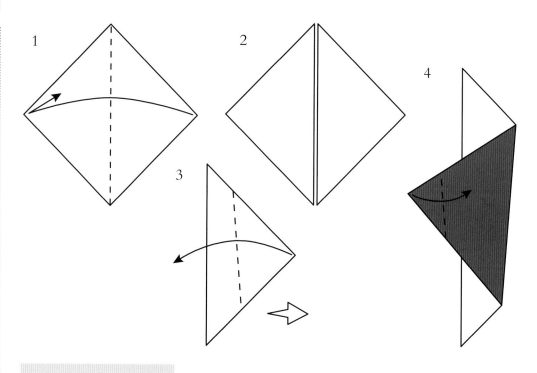

Materials

Unlike most traditional origami designs, Banana Boat needs only half a square; a square cut in half diagonally to form a 'silver' triangle. If you want to find out why this is the best paper shape to use for this design then try folding Banana Boat from a square and see what happens... A square of irogami and a small pair of scissors are needed.

Begin with your square arranged so that the white side is facing toward you.

1 Fold in half sideways, crease, then unfold.

2 Separate the triangles by cutting along the line of the crease.

3 Fold the right-hand point of the right-hand triangle across to the left as shown. Note that this crease is not parallel to the upright edge.

4 Fold the left-hand point inward a little.

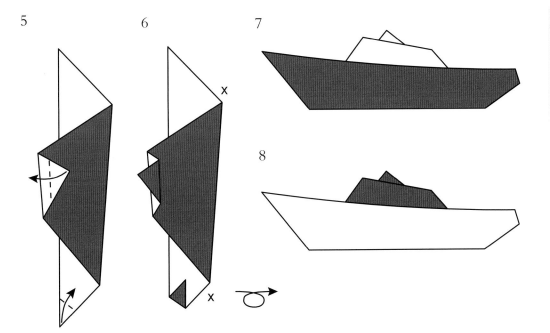

5   6   7

8

5 Make these two small folds to create the funnel and blunt the stern.

6 Pick the model up and curve gently by running your thumb nail along edge xx so that both bow and stern are bent slightly toward you. Turn over and align to Picture 7.

7 Banana Boat is finished. The curve of the hull not only suggests the flare of bow and stern but will also enable Banana Boat to stand upright if placed on a flat, level surface.

8 You can make a Banana Boat with a white hull and colored superstructure from the other triangle by starting with the paper 'colored side up.'

Unlocated Folds

Banana Boat is entirely different to Kabuto. In this design there are no location points for any of the folds. Folds made without location points are known as unlocated folds, judgement folds or, 'right about there' folds and must be made by eye alone. The advantage is that every time you fold the design it will come out slightly differently, while the disadvantage is that you can get it wrong. If you find it difficult to make unlocated folds by eye alone, you can check your angles by laying your paper on top of the diagrams as you fold.

The Banana Boat sketch can be brought to life by curving the hull (see Step 6). This not only suggests the flare of bow and stern but also enables Banana Boat to stand when placed gently on a smooth, flat surface. The curve is, of course, the reason for Banana Boat's name.

beginner

★

cormorant
on a rock

Cormorant on a Rock is a design that incorporates two separate elements, the cormorant and the rock, which are differentiated by a color change. The cormorant is formed from one surface of the paper and the rock from the other. The color change here is achieved using a reverse fold rather than the simple valley folds used in Banana Boat. Dual subjects like this are quite common in origami design and they can be extremely complex. Fortunately, this is one of the easiest to fold.

design: david mitchell

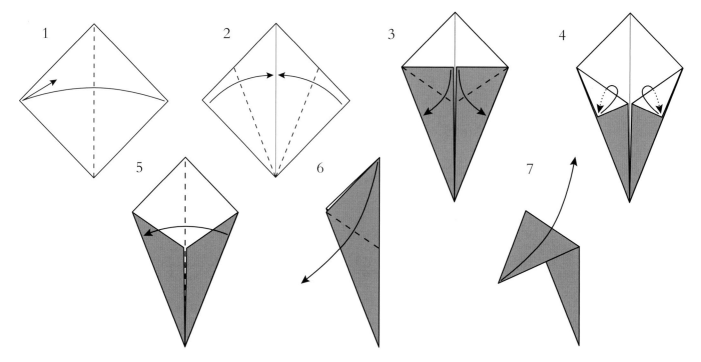

Materials

A single square of black/brown duo paper, black/white irogami, or any similar suitable color combination is required. Both surfaces of the paper are visible on the outside of the finished design.

Begin with your paper arranged so that the surface of the paper you want to form the Cormorant is facing away from you.

1 Fold in half sideways, crease, then unfold.

2 Fold both the bottom edges inward to lie along the crease made in Step 1, leaving a tiny gap between them. Try to make sure the point at the bottom remains sharp.

3 Fold the inside corners of the front flaps outward as shown.

4 Swing both front flaps out of sight by reversing the direction of the creases made in Step 3.

5 Fold the piece in half sideways.

6 Fold the top point down to the right, along the line of the edge of the internal layers.

7 Crease firmly, then open out the fold made in Step 6.

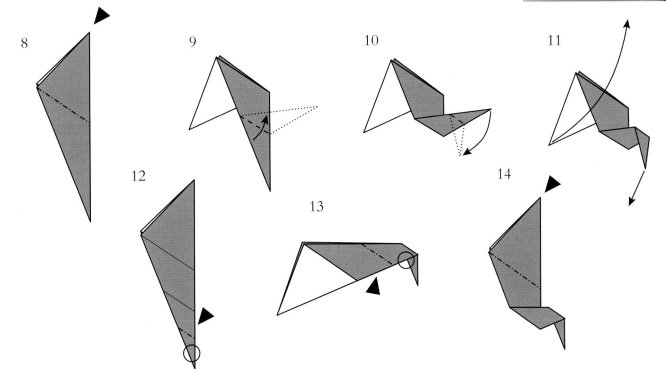

8 Turn the top point inside out between the other layers using the creases made in Step 6. You will have to reverse the direction of the crease made in the top layer of the paper as you do this. This kind of fold is called an inside reverse fold.

9 Fold the bottom point across to the right in the way shown here. There are no location points for this fold. You have to make it by eye so that it looks as much like Picture 10 as possible. It might help if you notice that the crease line is parallel to the sloping top right-hand edge.

10 Fold the right-hand point downward in a similar way.

11 Open out/undo the folds made in Steps 8 through 10.

12 This design can be created just using inside reverse folds like this. Hold the bottom point at the point marked with a circle and turn the rest of the design inside out using the crease made in Step 10.

13 Now hold the right-hand folds and turn the rest of the design inside out using the creases made in Step 9.

14 Repeat Step 8. Turn the top point inside out, etc.

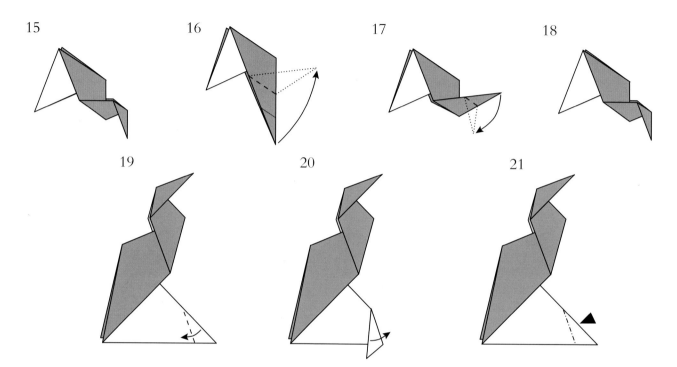

15   16   17   18

19   20   21

15 The more usual way of doing this would, however, be to use outside reverse folds. To practice this open back out to Step 9.

16 Turn the bottom point inside out outside the other layers using the creases made in Step 9. This is called an outside reverse fold.

17 Turn the right-hand point inside out outside the other layers using the creases made in Step 10.

18 The basic design is finished. Rotate and align with Picture 19 then follow instructions for 19 through 26 to add the fine details.

19 Begin to improve the rock the Cormorant is sitting on by folding over the tip of the right-hand point.

20 Open out the fold made in Step 19.

21 Inside reverse fold the right-hand point.

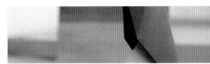

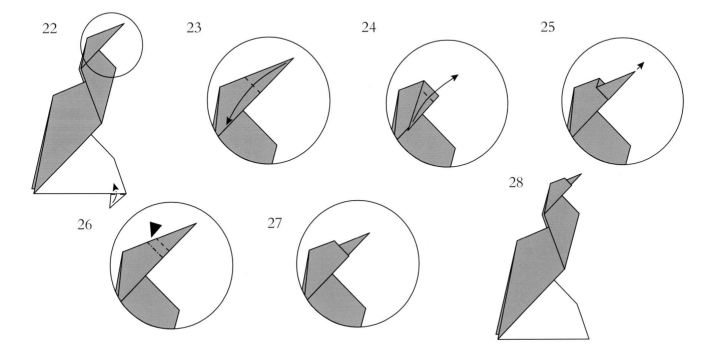

22   Fold the visible part of the flap away inside the design to lock the layers of the rock together. The enlargements will show how to improve the beak.

23   Fold the tip of the beak downward to the left like this.

24   Then back upward to the right.

25   Open out the folds made in Steps 23 and 24.

26   Separate the layers of the head and inside reverse fold the section of paper between the two fold lines out of sight inside the head leaving the beak sticking out.

27   The improved head and beak are finished.

28   The Cormorant on a Rock is finished, too. If you spread the layers at the bottom slightly, this design will stand up.

beginner

★

juxtaposition

Juxtaposition is an origami puzzle that is both created and solved by folding paper. The folding sequence uses a standard 4x4 grid to create a centerpiece and two endpieces which are cut out and then glued together to create the puzzle. The puzzle itself is in the form of a 3x1 rectangle. The rectangle is divided into three squares. Each square is crossed by diagonal creases. The challenge is to bring the endpieces together to form a series of simple juxtapositions of the endpieces by folding the strip in between, but only using the existing set of creases. Sounds easy...but is it?

design: david mitchell

Using Standard Grids

Many origami designs are developed from standard grids of creases which divide the starting square into smaller squares and triangles in a regular way. The most common standard grid is the 4x4 grid which divides the large square into 16 small squares. This grid is used as the basis of several designs in this book. Other designs you will come across use the less commonly encountered 3x3 grid. If you progress further with origami, you will meet other more esoteric standard grids, such as the 5x5 grid.

1

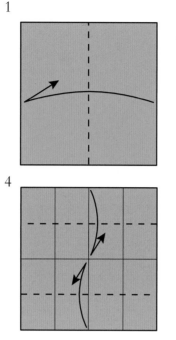

2

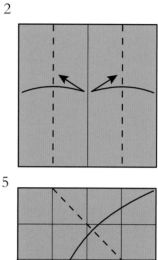

3

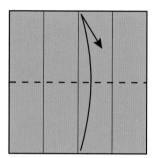

4

5

6

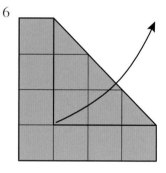

Materials

You will need two squares of paper the same size. One piece should be mono paper. The other can be of any type of paper. The two squares should be in distinctly different colors or patterns. You will also need a small pair of scissors and a gluestick or other similar adhesive.

Folding the centerpiece

The centerpiece is made from the mono square.

1 Fold in half sideways, crease, then unfold.

2 Fold both outside edges to the center, crease, then unfold.

3 Fold in half upward, crease, then unfold.

4 Fold the top and bottom edges to the center, crease, then unfold.

5 Fold the top right-hand corner inward as shown.

6 Open out the fold made in Step 5.

7

8

9

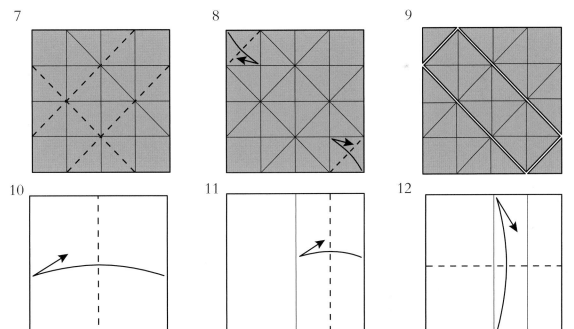

10

11

12

7 Repeat Folds 5 and 6 on the other three corners.

8 Fold two opposite small corner squares in half diagonally, crease, then unfold.

9 Cut off the four triangles around the central strip.

Folding the endpieces

The endpieces are made from the other mono or the irogami square. If you are using irogami begin with your square arranged white side up.

10 Fold in half sideways, crease, then unfold.

11 Fold the right edge into the center, crease, then unfold.

12 Fold in half upward, crease, then unfold.

Adding Decorations

Juxtaposition only works as a puzzle because the triangles at the end of the strip on both surfaces are made from different paper. In these circumstances, using glue to add decoration is clearly a valid method to adopt, although there are some paperfolders who regard both the use of glue and the addition of decoration as a breach of the pure origami ethic.

However, there comes a time when you need to step outside the rules and see what happens if you break them. In this spirit, you might like to think about how the Juxtaposition puzzle could be improved. Are other juxtapositions of the two triangles possible if the design is changed?
If so, where would you place additional creases to achieve them?

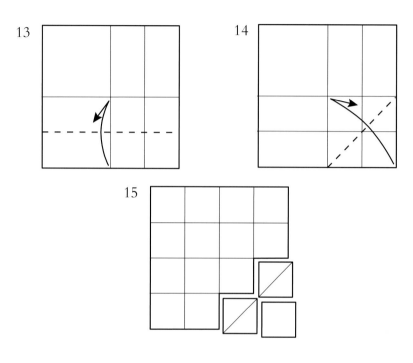

13 Fold the bottom edge into the center, crease, then unfold.

14 Fold the bottom right-hand corner into the center, crease, then unfold.

15 Cut out the two small squares that have a diagonal crease across them.

16

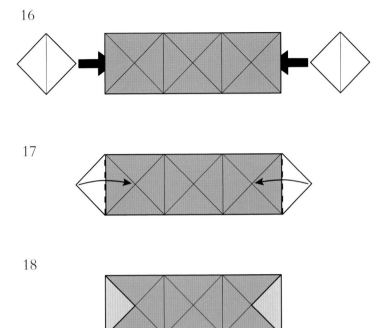

17

18

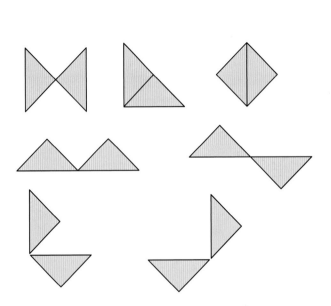

Attaching the endpieces

16 Cover the front surface of the small squares with adhesive and attach half of each to the back of the centerpiece as shown.

17 Fold the other half of the endpieces around in front and press down firmly.

18 Make sure all the creases fold freely in both directions. Juxtaposition is ready for use.

Attempting the challenge

Juxtaposition is a simple, manipulative puzzle. The challenge is to fold the paper, using only the existing creases, to juxtapose the endpieces in various ways. It's only the position of the endpieces that counts. You can have as much, or as little, of the centerpiece showing around them as you like. Can you achieve the juxtapositions shown above? Remember to be careful not to add any extra creases to the paper. Some are easy, some more difficult, but all are possible.

intermediate

★★

piranha

The Piranha is developed from the standard origami base known as the windmill base which is, in its turn, developed from a blintzed 4x4 grid. The windmill base can be developed to produce many other classic and traditional designs (such as the traditional Spanish 'little bird' known as the Pajarita). Piranha is also the first design in this book in which the fixed relationship between the different parts of the paper is used to create movement. Piranha's mouth opens and closes when the fins are manipulated. One of the wonders of origami is the ease with which it can be used to create action toys and models. The best action designs contain a simple mechanism which changes a small movement in one part of the paper into a surprisingly large movement in another. Try folding and operating Piranha and you will see.

design: david mitchell

Developing Traditional Bases

Bases are configurations of folds which allow for the further development of the paper. They are standard points of departure from which many origami journeys can be undertaken. Cormorant on a Rock was developed from the diamond base (shown in Picture 3). Piranha is developed from the windmill base. The set of standard bases is completed by the waterbomb base (Chinese Goldfish, page 66), the bird or crane base (Tsuru, page 50) and the fish and frog bases (neither used in this book).

Modern paperfolders have created many other bases, notably blintzed versions of the fish, bird and frog bases, but few of these provide as many points of departure, or lead to such a variety of finished designs as the traditional bases do in many different ways.

Materials

The Piranha can be folded from a square of any kind of paper but perhaps works best from thick mono. Both surfaces of the paper are visible on the outside of the finished design.

1
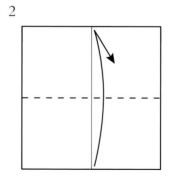

2
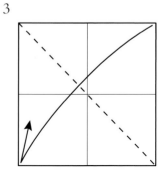

3
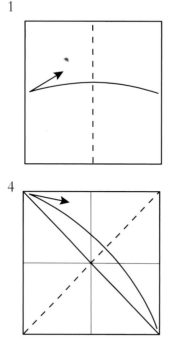

4
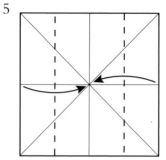

5
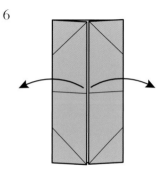

6

1 Fold in half sideways, crease, then unfold.

2 Fold in half upwards, crease, then unfold.

3 Fold in half diagonally, crease, then unfold.

4 Fold in half diagonally in the other direction, crease, then unfold.

5 Fold both the left- and right-hand edges into the center.

6 Open out the folds made in Step 5. Try to avoid flattening the creases as you do this.

7
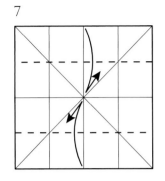

8
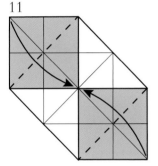

9
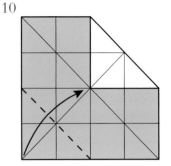

10
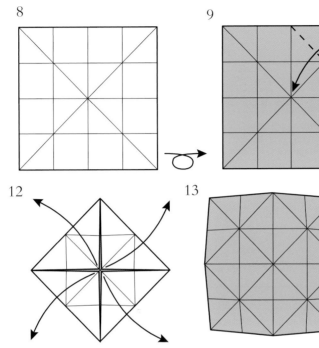

11

12

13

14
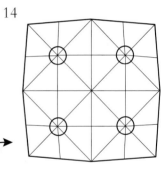

7 Fold the top and bottom edges into the center, crease, then unfold.

8 This is the result. Turn over.

9 Fold one corner into the center.

10 Fold the opposite corner into the center as well.

11 Fold the other two corners into the center, too. In technical origami language this process of folding all four corners of a square into the center is known as blintzing (see page 48).

12 Open out the folds made in Steps 9 through 11. Try to avoid flattening the creases as you do this.

13 This is the result. Turn over.

14 When you first turn the paper over, the four corners will be pointing slightly backward. Gently flip each corner forward in turn so that the intersections identified by circles become slightly concave.

Blintzing

Part of the process of creating the windmill base involves folding all four corners of the square into the center. This process is known as blintzing, and the resulting triangular flaps as blintzes.

Blintzing needs to be carried out as accurately as possible. The natural approach is often to fold in one corner and then work clockwise, or counterclockwise, around the rest, but this tends to magnify any inaccuracies. The approach explained in Steps 9 through 11 usually produces a better result.

15

16

17

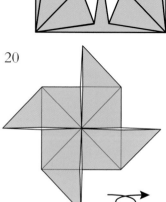

18

19

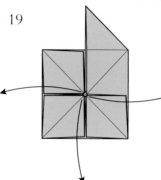

20

15 The result is a form like a shallow dish.

16 Fold the middle of each edge into the center of the dish.

17 Flatten the folds completely so that all the points marked with circles end up in the center.

18 This is the windmill base. Open out one flap to form one sail of the Windmill.

19 Open out the other three arms of the Windmill in a similar way.

20 This is the traditional design known as the Windmill. Turn over and rotate to align with Step 21.

21
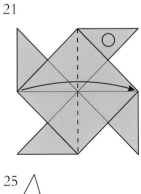

22
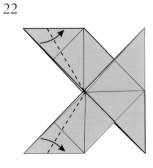

23

24

25
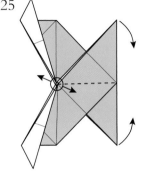

26

27

21 Pick the paper up and fold the top layers in half from left to right. Allow the flap marked with a circle to swing across to the left behind as you do this.

22 Fold the sloping left-hand edges of the mouth across to the right as shown. There are no location points for these folds. Try to ensure the top and bottom of the mouth remain as symmetrical as possible.

23 Open out the folds made in Step 22.

24 Outside reverse fold both flaps, using the creases made in Step 22, to form the mouth.

25 Take one of the tail-fins in each hand, rotate them so that they are at right-angles to the body, then ease the front of them gently apart so that the mouth opens. The result should look like Step 26.

26 As you do this the flap inside the mouth should swing to one side or the other. You will also need to remake the four creases around the mouth as mountain folds to reinforce the shape.

27 Piranha is finished. By holding the tail-fins and gently moving the tips slightly together and apart you can make the mouth open and close quite dramatically.

intermediate

★★

tsuru

The huge popularity of the Tsuru paperfold is due to its cultural associations rather than its intrinsic beauty. In Japan, the Tsuru is a traditional symbol of longevity and it is said that if you fold a thousand cranes you will live forever. Outside Japan, the Tsuru has become a symbol of good health, happiness and international peace. These modern associations have arisen as a result of the central part the folding of many Tsuru played in the story of Sadako Sasaki, a temporary survivor of the bombing of Hiroshima in 1945. Cranes are often now folded as gifts of hope for friends who are seriously ill, or as symbols of peace.

design: traditional japanese

Preliminary Fold

This base is derived from a simple configuration of folds known as the preliminary fold (Step 7). The preliminary fold can be used to show how a series of intersecting creases possess the ability to be configured in two different ways, without the necessity of reversing the creases, just by turning the intersection inside out. We can borrow and misuse a mathematical word and call these two configurations 'duals.'

The Tsuru, or Crane, is almost certainly the most famous and widely folded origami design ever. Judged purely as an origami design, though, the Tsuru lacks elegance. It is a difficult design to fold well because the thinning of the sides of the bird base creates points which are too thick to manipulate easily. Being able to fold the Tsuru well is a good test of a paperfolder's skill.

Materials

A single square of any kind of paper. Only one surface of the paper is visible on the outside of the finished design. If you are using duo paper or irogami, begin with your square arranged so that the surface you want to show on the outside of the design is facing toward you.

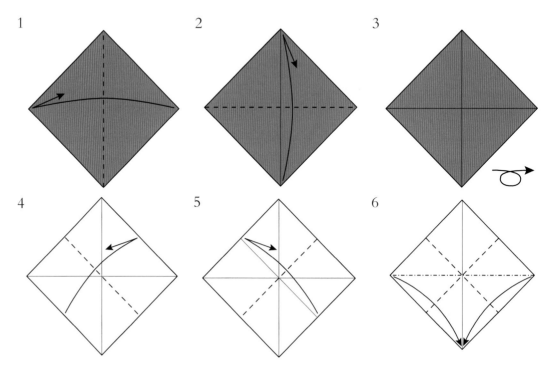

1 Fold in half sideways, crease, then unfold.

2 Fold in half upwards, crease, then unfold.

3 Turn the piece over.

4 Fold in half diagonally from edge to edge as shown, crease, then unfold.

5 Fold in half diagonally from edge to edge in the other direction, crease, then unfold.

6 Bring all four corners together at the bottom. The square will collapse into the form shown in Step 7.

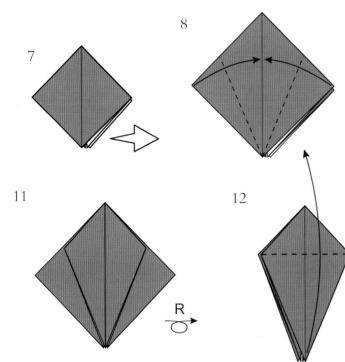

7

8

9

10

11

12

R

13

14

7 Step 8 shows this form on a larger scale.

8 This form, known as the preliminary fold, is one of the traditional bases of origami from which many other bases and designs have been developed. Carefully fold the outside edges of the two front flaps inward so that they meet along the vertical center crease. Try to make sure that you get sharp points at the bottom.

9 Open out the folds made in Step 8.

10 Inside reverse fold the outside edges of the front flaps. You will need to reverse the direction of the creases in the front layer as you do this.

11 Turn over and repeat Steps 8 through 10 on the other half of the paper. The result should look like Step 12.

12 This is the Bird Base. Fold the front flap upward.

13 Turn the piece over.

14 Fold the new front flap upward in the same way.

The Bird Base

The bird base, the standard base from which the Tsuru is developed, has been called the greatest achievement of traditional Japanese origami and there is a good deal of justification for this opinion. The reason is that it possesses four points, each of which can be developed and manipulated with a great deal of freedom.

Four points is a useful number to have available. If you are modeling a bird, four points will give you two wings, a head and a tail, or two legs, a head and a tail, if you prefer.

Modelling animals generally requires a few more. A short tail can generally be developed without using an entire point, but one is certainly required for the head, and legs usually require one each as well. Five points are hard to find from a square, which explains why the bird base has been developed into so many designs for three-legged origami animals.

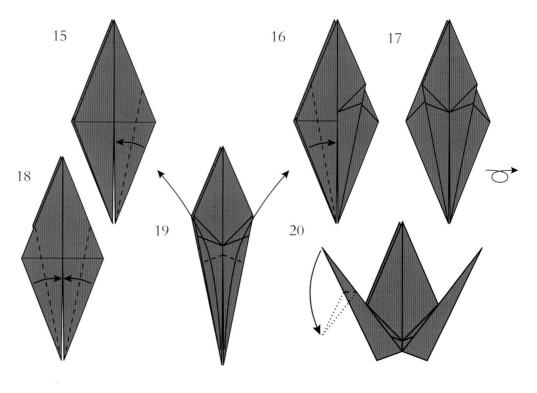

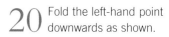

15 Fold the sloping right-hand edge of the front layer inwards to lie on the vertical center crease.

16 Repeat Fold 15 on the left-hand side of the design.

17 Turn the piece over.

18 Repeat Folds 15 and 16 on the other half of the paper.

19 Fold both the points at the bottom upward as far as they will go. Step 20 shows what the result should look like.

20 Fold the left-hand point downwards as shown.

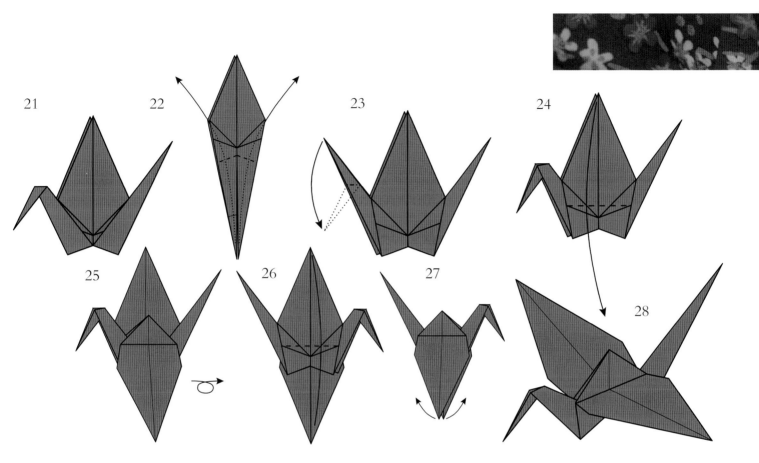

21   22   23   24

25   26   27   28

21 Crease firmly then undo the folds made in Steps 19 and 20.

22 Inside reverse fold the bottom flaps upward using the creases made in Step 19.

23 Inside reverse fold the head downward using the creases made in Step 20.

24 Fold the front wing downward as far as it will go.

25 Turn the piece over.

26 Fold the other wing downward in the same way.

27 Lift the wings up at right-angles in front and behind.

28 Spread the layers at the base of the tail slightly so that the Crane will stand.

intermediate

★★

clingons

Clingons are a simple design, developed from the bird base, that can be combined into hanging chains without the use of needle and thread. As a design, they are more geometric than representational, but you can also see them as evocative of robotic aliens descending from a starship onto a barren landscape. The angles at which the arms are folded allow each Clingon to hang suspended from the one above. What the top one hangs from is open to the imagination. A skyhook, perhaps? The most I have managed to hang in one chain is a mere 25.

design: david mitchell

Combining Finished Designs

Many finished designs can be combined to create mobiles and sculptures. Origami designs are ideal for use in mobiles because provided they are all folded from the same type, size and shape of paper, all the designs will be the same weight and consequently easy to balance against each other. The idea of combination designs is not new. In Japan it is traditional to create garlands of Tsuru, or cranes (see page 50) by threading them together. You can string them into garlands by threading a needle up through the center of each design in turn. If you are making and threading together the traditional thousand cranes, it is probably wise both to use very strong thread and to only put a hundred or so cranes onto the same garland. You can join the garlands together at a later stage. The effect is sublime.

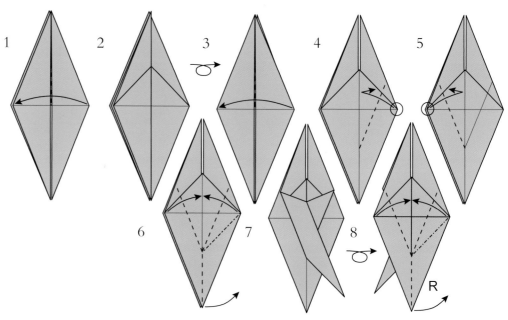

Materials

A single square of any kind of paper can be used. Clingons work best if folded from medium-weight paper. Only one surface of the paper is visible on the outside of the finished design.

Begin by folding your square to Step 15 of the Tsuru.

1 Fold the front layers in half sideways.

2 Turn the piece over.

3 Fold the new front layers in half sideways in the same way.

4 Fold the corner of the front layers marked with a circle onto the vertical center crease, so that the new crease is parallel to the sloping bottom right-hand edge. Make sure the new crease stops at the vertical center crease.

5 Check your new crease is in the right place then repeat Fold 4 on the left-hand side of the design.

6 Remake Folds 4 and 5 in that order, then swing the front bottom point across to the right and flatten so that it looks like Step 7. You will create two new creases as you do this. Take your time getting this right.

7 Turn the piece over.

8 Repeat Folds 4 through 6 on this side of the design.

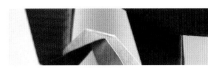

9

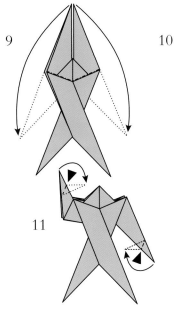

10

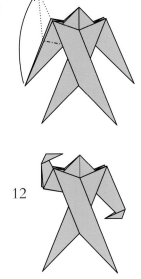

11

12

13

9 Inside reverse fold both arms downwards along the lines of the top of the shoulders.

10 Inside reverse fold the left arm upward as shown.

11 Outside reverse fold the tips of both arms to form hands.

12 Your first Clingon is finished. Make several more.

13 Because of the way the hands are positioned, Clingons can be arranged to form hanging chains, as if, perhaps, they were alien robots descending from a starship.

Process Focused

Clingons are a good example of a design developed by following the possibilities offered by the paper rather than by manipulating the paper to achieve a particular result. Process focused design is more than just origami 'doodling.' It is a quite deliberate exploration to find out what further possibilities exist in one particular configuration of folds — in this case the bird base — and then to develop the potential these possibilities offer into a new design. The alternative design strategy is result focused design, in which the designer starts with a result in mind then attempts to work out a folding strategy to achieve it, often nowadays using complex mathematical analyses. Both design methods are completely valid, and both have their advantages, but process focused design tends, on average, to produce more original and elegant results.

intermediate
★★

lover's knot

Lover's Knots were originally the name given to folds of various types which were intended to keep a letter safe from interference, or at least to ensure that if the letter had been opened and read, the recipient could tell that this had happened. For fairly obvious reasons, the name has long been applied to this traditional Japanese paperfold. This appears to be a romantic Western interpretation and there is no evidence that this was its original intention or purpose. Lover's Knot uses a technique known as the pull-out squash, which can also be used to turn the traditional Tsuru into a Flying Crane.

design: traditional japanese

The Pull-out Squash

This is a maneuver that is little used in modern origami design but is relatively common in the repertoire of traditional designs. The pull-out squash maneuver flattens a point to a rounded cushion-like surface or a flat square. In the case of the Flying Crane the point that is pulled apart and squashed is clearly visible. In the case of the Lover's Knot it is hidden inside the folds.

In Japan the Tsuru is usually folded in the way shown in picture 28 of the Tsuru diagrams (see page 50), but in the West it is more common to finish it off by pulling the wings apart in a pull-out squash move to create a three-dimensional cushion-like effect. In this form the design is sometimes called the Flying Crane.

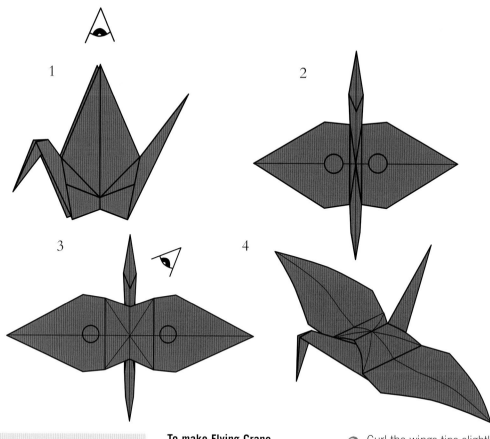

Materials

A single square of any kind of paper. Only one surface of the paper is visible on the outside of the finished design.

To make Flying Crane

Begin with Step 25 of the Tsuru.

1 The next picture is drawn as if viewed from above.

2 Take hold of a wing in each hand, holding them close to the body at the points marked by circles, and gently pull your hands apart. The body of the crane will open out until it looks like Step 27. Don't flatten the body completely.

3 Curl the wings tips slightly downward to complete the Flying Crane.

4 The Flying Crane is finished.

1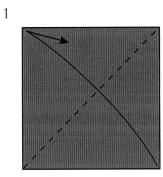

2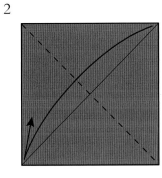

3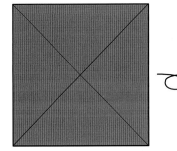

4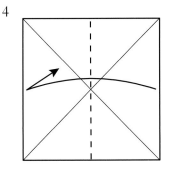

5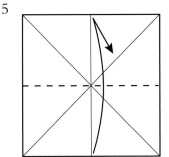

6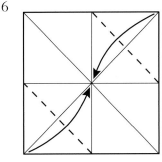

7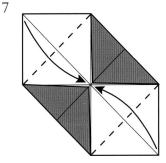

Materials

A single square of any kind of paper. Both surfaces of the paper are visible on the outside of the finished design. If using duo paper, or irogami, begin with your square arranged so that the surface you want to form the outside of the knot is facing away from you.

To make Lover's Knot

1 Fold in half diagonally, crease, then unfold.

2 Fold in half diagonally in the other direction, crease, then unfold.

3 Turn the piece over.

4 Fold in half from right to left, crease, then unfold.

5 Fold in half from bottom to top, crease, then unfold.

6 Fold two opposite corners to the center.

7 Fold the remaining corners into the center as well. This is known as blintzing.

Double Blintzing

The Lover's Knot is made by blintzing a square, turning it over and blintzing it again. This is a common technique in traditional paperfolding. Multiple blintzing is also used to create the possibilities that are developed in such designs as the well-known Fortune Teller (or Saltcellar), Yakkosan (or the Man-servant) and the traditional Water Lily fold for a napkin or serviette.

Fortune Teller

Yakkosan

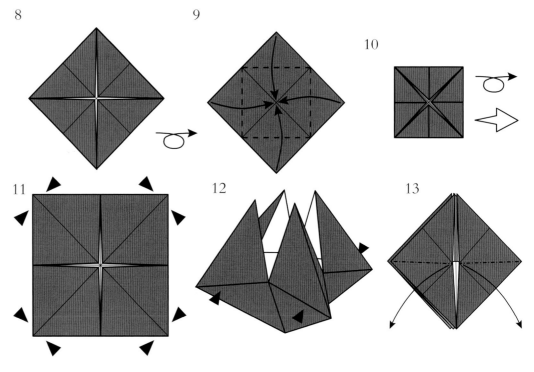

8 Turn over.

9 Blintz this smaller square as well. Your folds will be more accurate if you fold opposite, rather than adjacent corners inward first.

10 Turn over. The next picture is on a larger scale.

11 Squeeze the corners together. As you do this make sure the front layers move towards you and the back layers move away.

12 This picture shows this move in progress. Squeeze the corners together completely, then flatten the design so that it looks like Step 13.

13 Open the front flaps at the centre and squash fold them downwards. Step 14 shows what the result should look like.

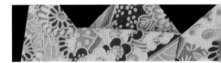

14

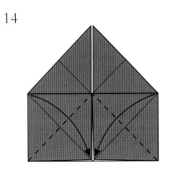

15

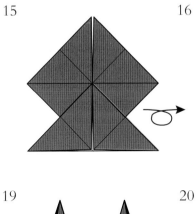

16

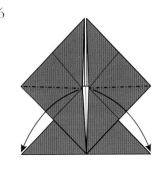

17

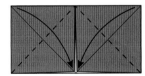

18

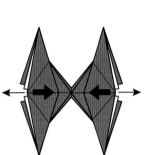

19

20

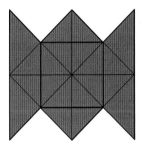

21

14 Fold the top corners of the front layer inwards as shown. Crease firmly.

15 Turn the piece over.

16 Repeat Fold 13 on the other half of the paper.

17 Now repeat Fold 14 as well.

18 The next picture shows the design from a different viewpoint.

19 Insert your thumbs into the pockets marked with arrows and gently pull them apart.

20 As you do this, the central spike will flatten. This picture shows the process part way through. Keep flattening the spike until it becomes a completely flat square.

21 The Lover's Knot is finished.

intermediate

★ ★

chinese goldfish

There is a distinct, and distinctive, paperfolding tradition in China that is called zhe zhi (Mandarin) rather than origami. The Chinese tradition mainly consists of the folding of Yuen Bao, which are paper representations of gold or silver ingots to be burned at funerals and in memory of the ancestors, and of representations of auspicious animals such as tortoises, rabbits and even goldfish. The Chinese Goldfish is a traditional Chinese design that appears to have been developed from the traditional paperfold known in the West as the water bomb.

design: traditional chinese

Inflatable Areas

One distinctive aspect of the Chinese tradition is the way in which many designs are first folded flat but then opened up into a three-dimensional form at the very end of the folding sequence. This is achieved using several different techniques, but notably the pull-out squash and the use of inflatable areas. These are also used in the Japanese tradition.

The Chinese Goldfish is a traditional design that appears to have been developed from the water bomb (so called because it can be filled with water and thrown) or in Japan as the Balloon. To fold the water bomb you fold to Step 10, turn the design over, and then repeat Folds 7 through 9 on the other half. The result of inflating the model is a cube with rounded corners. The design of the Chinese Goldfish is more sophisticated, but it is correspondingly harder to inflate.

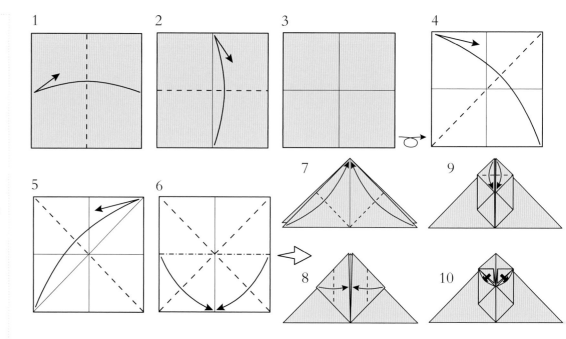

Materials

A single square of any kind of paper. Only one surface of the paper is visible on the outside of the finished design.

1 Fold in half sideways, crease, then unfold.

2 Fold in half upward, crease, then unfold.

3 Turn the piece over.

4 Fold in half diagonally, crease, then unfold.

5 Fold in half diagonally in the alternate direction, crease, then unfold.

6 Collapse into a water bomb base.

7 Fold both front corners up to the top.

8 Fold the outside corners of the front layers inward to lie on the vertical edges of the flaps. Try to keep your new creases parallel to these edges.

9 Fold the tips of the top flaps in half downward to form double flaps.

10 Tuck both double flaps away into the pockets below them. Crease firmly.

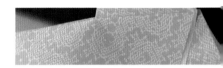

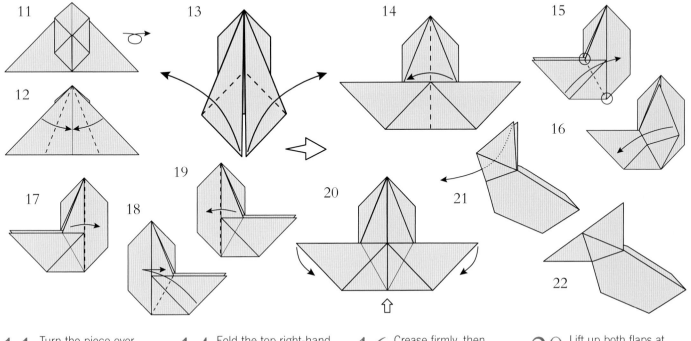

11 Turn the piece over.

12 Fold both sloping edges onto the vertical center crease.

13 Fold the tips of both flaps outward as shown. When you have done this, the top of the flaps should form a straight horizontal line.

14 Fold the top right-hand layers across to the left.

15 Fold the top left-hand layer back across to the right using the points marked with circles to locate the crease.

16 Crease firmly, then unfold.

17 Fold both front flaps across to the right.

18 Repeat Steps 15 and 16 in the opposite direction.

19 Fold the front flap back across to the left.

20 Lift up both flaps at right-angles to the base and inflate by blowing gently in the hole at the bottom.

21 Flip the front fin downward between the layers to complete the tail.

22 The Chinese Goldfish is finished.

intermediate

★★

fish bowl

The Japanese Goldfish (left) is a traditional development
of the Kabuto, effected by the help of two small,
strategically-placed cuts. The Koi Carp (not shown) is
a modern design developed in exactly the same way.
It goes to show that even the Japanese sometimes
overlook the obvious. The Knotfish (right) is a simple fish
developed from the Lover's Knot. You will recognize the
mouth from the Piranha, although this particular design
is not an action model.

design: japanese traditional / david mitchell

Simple Transformations

It is often possible to transmute an existing origami design into a new one. There are sets of designs that develop from each other in the traditional repertoire, particularly in the Japanese tradition. These transformations may well have been happy accidents, or they may have been the result of some intentional exploration of possibilities. The origins of many of these folds are lost in time and these transformations are not always fish... although there does appear to be a theme developing.

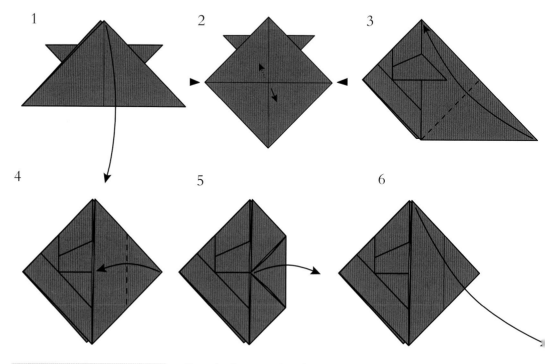

Materials

For all three fish — a single square of mono paper and a small pair of scissors are needed. Both surfaces of the paper are visible on the outside of the finished design.

To make Japanese Goldfish

Complete Steps 1-11 of the Kabuto (see page 24).

1 Swing the front layer downward.

2 Squeeze the left- and right-hand corners toward each other so that the center opens up in front and behind. Continue squeezing until the corners meet in the center. The result should look like Step 3.

3 Fold the right-hand point inward and upward using the existing crease.

4 Fold the right-hand point into the center.

5 Undo the fold made in Step 4.

6 Undo the fold made in Step 3.

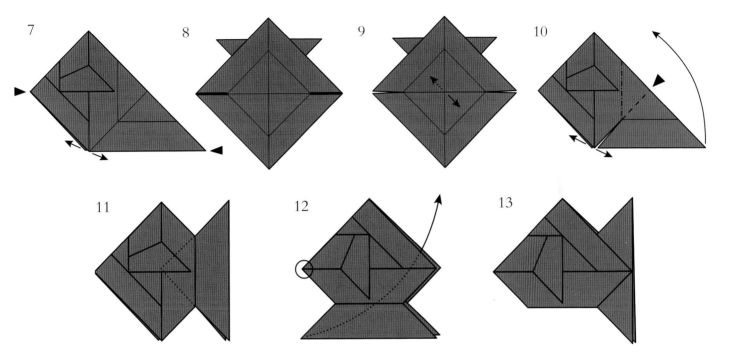

7 Squeeze the left- and right-hand corners toward each other so that the center opens up in front and behind.

8 Cut along the creases marked with a thick black line. Make sure you only cut through the front layer of the paper.

9 Squeeze the left- and right-hand corners toward each other so that the center opens up in front and behind. Continue squeezing until the corners meet in the center. The result should look like Step 10.

10 Separate the front and back layers then gently push the triangular areas on either side of the push symbol completely inside out. As you do this the right-hand point will flip upward.

11 This is the result. The dotted line shows the position of the darker shaded area of paper shown in Step 10 after the maneuver has been completed. The Japanese Goldfish is finished.

To make Koi Carp

Begin with the Japanese Goldfish. Align the design with Step 12.

12 With your left hand take hold of the Japanese Goldfish at the point marked with a circle. Now use your right hand to turn the tail completely inside out between the other layers. This can be done in one smooth move.

13 Voilà! The Koi Carp is finished.

Using Cuts

While the use of cuts was common in the Japanese tradition of origami it is almost anathema to many modern paperfolders. This is partly because it goes against the pure origami ethic, and partly because it alters the paper's interconnectedness, which makes the origami design process much less challenging. While it is better to avoid cuts if you can, there is a point at which avoiding them becomes so inelegant that the use of a few judicious cuts to simplify the design can be totally justified. You might like to work out for yourself how to fold the Japanese Goldfish without using cuts. Which method is more elegant and which is better overall?

Another use of cuts is to partly sub-divide a large sheet of paper into smaller individual, but still connected, sheets which can then be folded into a more complex design (see page 148).

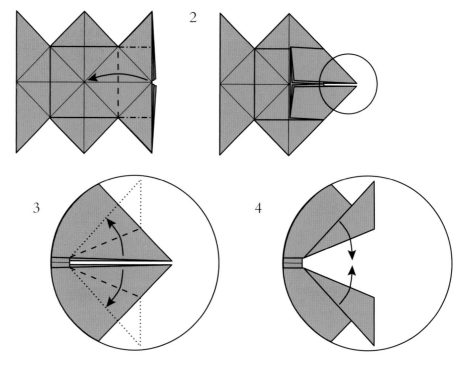

To make Knotfish

Complete Steps 1-21 of the Lover's Knot (see page 60).

1 Fold the center of the front two layers of the right-hand edge to the left and flatten so that the design looks like Step 2.

2 The enlargements show how to form the mouth.

3 Fold the lips upward and downward as shown.

4 Open out the folds made in Step 3.

5

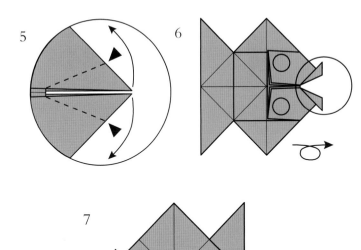

6

7

5 Outside reverse fold the lips. You will be able to open out the flaps marked with small circles in Picture 6 to make this easier to achieve.

6 Turn the project over.

7 The Knotfish is finished.

intermediate
★★

flapping parrot

The Flapping Parrot is a development of a design known as Merlin's Bird, which was folded from a rhombus. Changing the starting shape to a square provided sufficient paper to change a rather generic bird into a recognizable parrot and to provide it not only with an excellent flapping action but also the ability to perch on the edge of a box or table. The design also makes excellent use of a color change. If you fold the Flapping Parrot from irogami or, even better, from duo paper, the white surface, or, in the case of duo paper, the second color, will flash into view as you manipulate the design to make the wings flap.

design: david mitchell

Beyond Standard Bases

The representational designs so far have mostly been folded from standard bases: Cormorant from the diamond base, Piranha from the windmill base, Tsuru from the bird base, and the Chinese Goldfish from the water bomb base. The Flapping Parrot is different. It is designed around a mechanism rather than a base, though the basic principle of representational origami design, that excess paper is used as effectively as possible to add detail to the design, is maintained.

There was a time when most new origami designs were manipulated from standard bases. Modern paperfolding designers tend to either dispense with bases altogether or to design their own custom bases for each individual design in order to provide the right number of manipulable points, in the right relationship, to allow them to develop the design they have in mind.

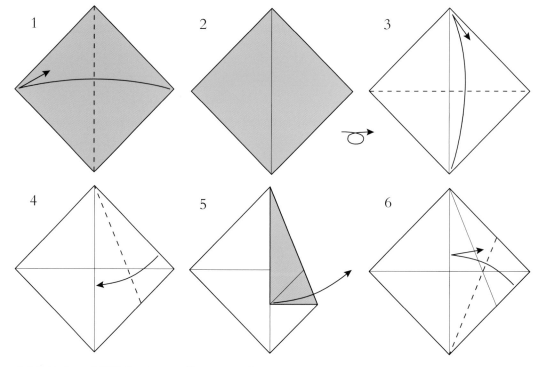

Materials

A single square of any kind of paper. Thin paper works best. Both surfaces of the paper are visible on the outside of the finished design.

If you are using duo paper, or irogami, begin with the surface you want to show on the outside of the design facing toward you.

1 Fold in half sideways, crease, then unfold.

2 Turn the piece over.

3 Fold in half upward, crease, then unfold.

4 Fold the top, sloping right-hand edge onto the vertical center crease.

5 Crease as shown, then unfold.

6 Repeat Folds 4 and 5 on the bottom sloping right-hand edge, crease, then unfold.

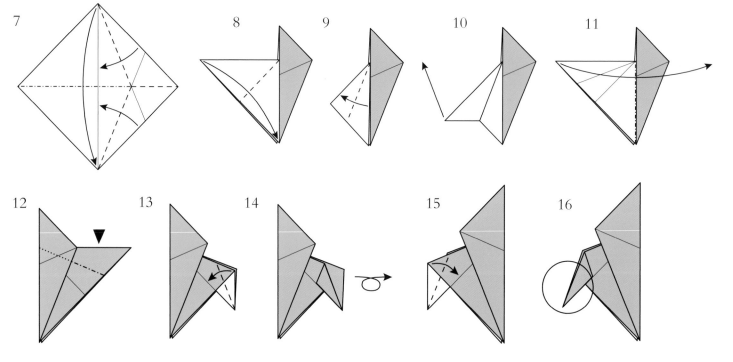

7 You will need to pick the paper up to make this fold. Fold the paper in half backward while allowing the folds made in Steps 4 through 6 to reform. The result should look like Picture 8.

8 Fold the left-hand point in half, inward, like this.

9 Fold the front flap in half again, outward, as shown.

10 Crease, then pull the left-hand point upward to open out the folds made in Steps 8 and 9.

11 Pick the paper up again and fold the left-hand point to the right in between the layers.

12 Inside reverse fold the right-hand point down in between the layers using the crease made in Step 9.

13 Fold the front layer of the right-hand point in half.

14 Turn the piece over.

15 Repeat Fold 13 on this side of the design.

16 The enlargements show how to form the head and beak.

That Sinking Feeling

By this point in the book you will already be completely at home with inside and outside reverse folds, both of which are made in a point which has an open edge. There is a further kind of reverse fold which is made in a point which has no open edge and which is known as a sink. Sinks come in two varieties, open and closed. Open sinks are relatively easy to make. Closed sinks can be fiendishly difficult. Fortunately the sink needed to make the Flapping Parrot (see Step 25) is of the easy, open variety.

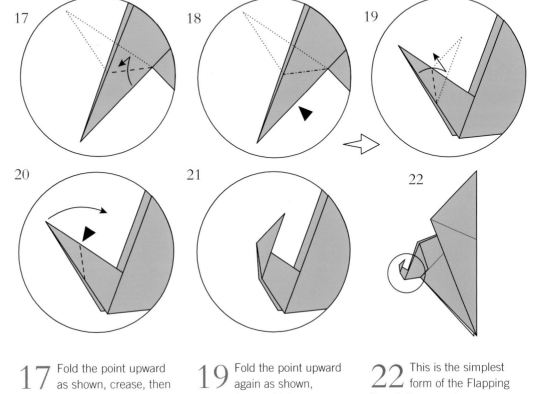

17 Fold the point upward as shown, crease, then unfold.

18 Inside reverse fold the point to form the head using the creases made in Step 17.

19 Fold the point upward again as shown, crease, then unfold.

20 Outside reverse fold to form the beak.

21 This is what the result should look like. Adjust if necessary.

22 This is the simplest form of the Flapping Parrot. If you prefer you can go straight to Step 31 now, or follow Steps 23 to 29 to create a more sophisticated bird.

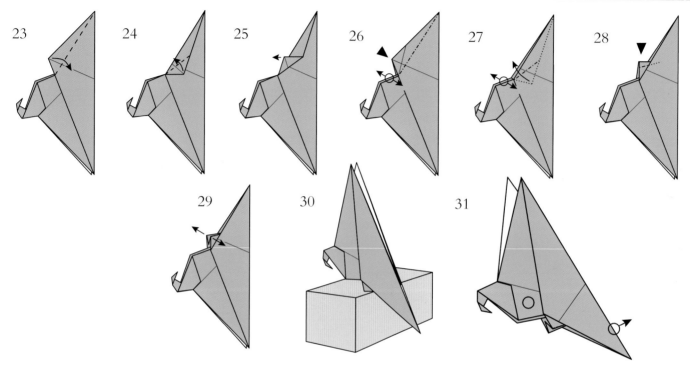

23 Fold the sloping edge of the top point inward as shown.

24 Fold the obtuse point of the front flap outward again so that the result looks like Step 25.

25 Open out the folds made in Steps 23 and 24.

26 Open out the layers at the point marked with a circle and turn the sloping edge of the top point inside out between them. In technical origami language this kind of inside reverse fold, which does not affect an open edge, is known as an open sink.

27 Open out the folds at the point marked with a circle and pull out the small flap inside using the creases made in Step 24.

28 Inside reverse fold the tip of the new flap to separate the feet.

29 Gently separate the feet and rotate the design to align it with Step 30.

30 The Flapping Parrot will perch on the edge of a small box.

31 To make the Flapping Parrot flap, hold the front layers together at the point marked with a circle and gently pull the tail upward to the right.

intermediate
★★

tato

Tato is a Japanese word for a folding purse. In origami it is sometimes (mis)used to refer to any geometric design which has rotational symmetry. This particular Tato is of interest because of the way in which the star pattern is produced on the front surface as the edges of the paper are interwoven in the center, and because it uses root 5 geometry, something that is very unusual in a traditional design. Tato is an ideal design to send you hunting through your local shops to find the perfect paper to fold it from. Paperfolders spend long hours in this happy pursuit.

design: traditional japanese

Altering the Angles

Up to this point, all the designs in this book have been created using the same system of basic angles. Right-angles (90°) have been folded in half to produce angles of 45° which in turn have been folded in half to produce angles of 22.5° and so on. Just occasionally, judgement folds have involved you in folding the paper at other unspecified angles but the possibilities inherent in alternative angular systems have not been explored.

This changes here. Tato uses root 5 geometry, Give Me Sunshine uses the geometry of the 3:4:5 right-angle triangle, Shipwreck uses 60° geometry and Artifact and Stargate explore the possibilities of the geometry of the 1:root2 or 'silver rectangle.' All this is much less challenging than it sounds. You will hardly notice the mathematics as you fold, but it will be there all the same.

1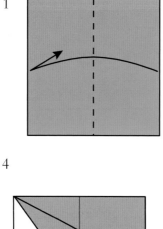

2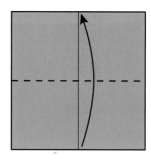

3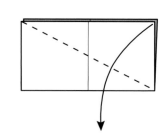

4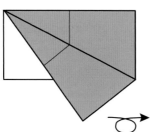

5

6

Materials

A single square of irogami or duo paper. Both surfaces of the paper are visible on the outside of the finished design.

Begin with your square arranged so that the surface of the paper you want to form the outside of the Tato is facing toward you. The other surface will form the inside and the star.

1 Fold in half sideways, crease, then unfold.

2 Fold the piece in half upward.

3 Fold the front layer in half diagonally downward as shown, making sure the crease begins and ends exactly at the corners.

4 Turn the piece over.

5 Repeat the fold explained in Step 3 on the new front layer.

6 Open out the folds made in Steps 3 through 5.

7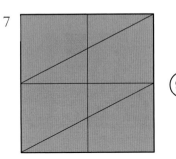

8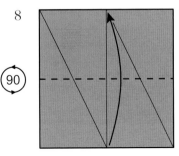

9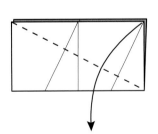

10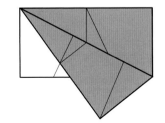

11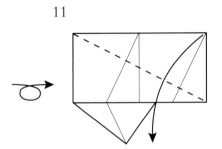

12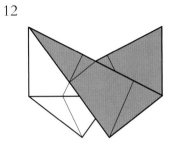

13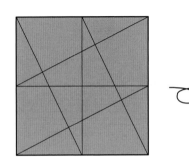

7 Rotate through 90°.

8 Fold the square in half upwards.

9 Fold the front layer in half diagonally downwards as shown, making sure the crease begins and ends exactly at the corners.

10 Turn the piece over.

11 Repeat the fold from Step 5.

12 Open out the folds made in Steps 9 through 11.

13 Check that you have made all the creases shown in this picture. Turn over.

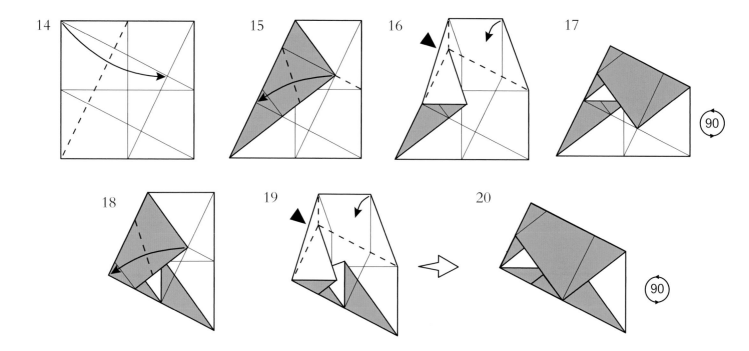

14 Fold the top left corner inward using the existing crease.

15 Make the fold shown in the front layer only. The design will become three-dimensional at this point.

16 Gently push the smaller of the two upright flaps inward as shown, then fold the larger upright flap down on top of it. You will create a new crease between the layers as you do this.

17 Check your design looks like this, then rotate the piece 90° counterclockwise.

18 Repeat Fold 15 in the new front layer.

19 Repeat Fold 16 to flatten the upright flaps. The next picture is on a larger scale.

20 Check your design looks like this, then rotate 90° counterclockwise.

21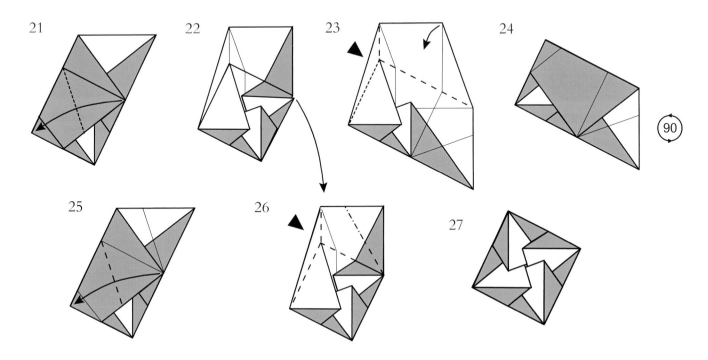

22

23

24

25

26

27

21 Repeat Fold 15 in the new front layer.

22 Pull out the layers at the right-hand side.

23 Repeat Fold 16 to flatten the upright flaps.

24 Check your design looks like this, then rotate 90° counterclockwise.

25 Repeat Fold 15 in the new front layer.

26 Repeat Fold 16 to flatten the upright flaps, but as you do so, also remake the folds made in Steps 15 and 16. The result will look like Step 27.

27 The finished Tato looks like this. You can open it by pulling gently on the point of the top layers of two opposite corners.

give me sunshine

Give Me Sunshine is a subtle bas-relief representation of the sun and its rays. It is both a geometric and a representational design and definitely blurs the boundaries. Essentially the design is made from a series of criss-crossing creases that allow themselves to be gently collapsed into the form of a shallow dish where the tension between the creases holds the form in equilibrium. With a little experimentation you will find that Give Me Sunshine will also collapse into a second state of equilibrium, a somewhat deeper bowl. In the original shallow dish form, Give Me Sunshine will stand upright on any edge. You could also display it inside a suitably-sized shallow box or lid. Sunglasses on!

design: david mitchell

Crease and Collapse Designs

Most simple origami designs are made in a series of progressive steps that create the design, so that first the basic form and then the detail gradually appears. All the designs you have folded so far in this book are of this progressive type. There is, however, a second category of origami designs which are created in an entirely different way. As the name suggests, crease and collapse designs are made in two stages. In the first stage a series of intersecting creases are set into the paper, and their correct directions through the paper are established. In the second stage, these creases are used to collapse the paper into a different form.

Here the collapse is used to create not just the base but the finished design itself, effectively all in one go. Similar crease and collapse techniques are used later in this book.

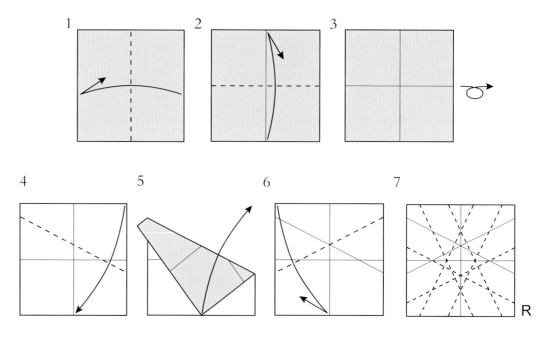

Materials

A single square of paper with one yellow surface (unless you want a bright blue sun, of course). Medium weight paper works better. Both surfaces of the paper are visible on the outside of the finished design but they are not mixed.

If you are using duo paper, or irogami, begin with the yellow surface facing toward you.

1 Fold in half sideways, crease, then unfold.

2 Fold in half upwards, crease, then unfold.

3 Turn the piece over.

4 Fold the top right-hand corner onto the center of the bottom edge.

5 Crease the paper firmly, then unfold.

6 Fold the top left-hand corner onto the center of the bottom edge, crease, then unfold.

7 Repeat Steps 4 through 6 by folding both corners of the other three sides to the middle of the opposite edges to form the additional creases shown here.

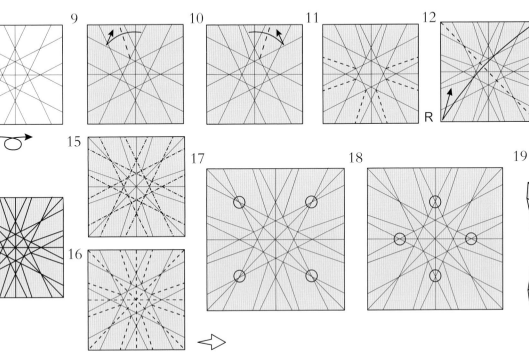

8 Check that the pattern of creases you have made looks like this. Turn over.

9 Make a short, new crease in the way shown here. Make sure that this crease only goes part way across the paper.

10 Make a similar crease on the right-hand side of the paper.

11 Make six more creases in a similar way.

12 Fold in half diagonally, crease, then unfold.

13 Fold in half diagonally in the alternate direction, crease, then unfold.

14 The pre-creasing phase is finished. The collapse will only work if all the creases are sharp and correctly assigned as either mountain or valley folds.

15 These are the mountain folds.

16 And these are the valley folds. The next picture is on a larger scale.

17 To collapse the design, gently squeeze the points marked with circles so that they rise up toward you. Make sure you maintain all the mountain/valley assignments. A sun-shaped shallow bowl should start to form in the center as you do this.

18 Finish forming Give Me Sunshine by gently squeezing these points together as well. When you let go, the tension in the creases should hold the design in its finished three-dimensional form.

19 Give Me Sunshine will stand upright on one edge, or can be framed in a suitably-sized box or lid.

beginner

★

egypt

Egypt is a minimalist landscape created by using the contrast between the two surfaces of irogami or duo paper to draw a sketch of the pyramids. Two versions of the design are given. The first version, folded directly from a square, is simple to fold, but the pyramids are set too far apart, one at each edge of the paper. In the second version, the pyramids are close together, indeed they overlap, but the design is a little more difficult to fold. The improvement between the versions is achieved by changing the starting shape from a square to a 3x4 rectangle.

design: david mitchell

Changing the Starting Shape

Almost all the designs so far have been folded from squares. Squares are undoubtedly the most popular starting shape for origami designs and some designers use them to the virtual exclusion of any other shape. There is even a school of thought within origami, that pure origami should only be about folding from squares. Squares certainly do have some advantages over other paper shapes; better symmetry, the ease with which it is possible to construct the location points for many angular systems and the fact that designs can be laid out on the diagonal.

But other starting shapes, particularly other rectangles, have their advantages too. They can be used to vary the proportions of the design to improve its artistic qualities or verisimilitude, or to facilitate the elegant development of alternative folding geometries.

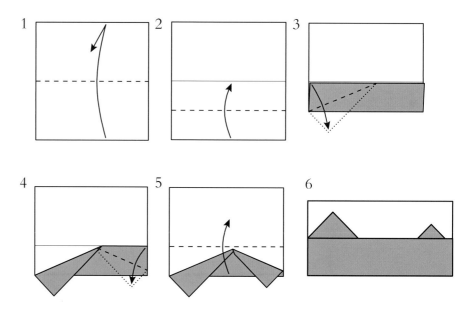

Materials

Each version requires a single square of duo or irogami paper. Both surfaces of the paper are visible on the outside of the finished design.

Version 1

You will need a square of duo or irogami paper. Begin with the side of the paper you wish to form the sky facing toward you.

1 Fold in half upward, crease, then unfold.

2 Fold the bottom edge up to the horizontal center crease.

3 Fold the top left-hand corner of the front flap downward to form the first Pyramid. Try to make sure that both sides of the Pyramid slope at the same 45° angle.

4 Create a second, smaller, Pyramid in a similar way.

5 Fold the bottom layers upwards using the crease made in Step 1.

6 The basic version of Egypt is finished. Now follow Steps 7 through 13 to see how much the design can be improved by changing the starting shape.

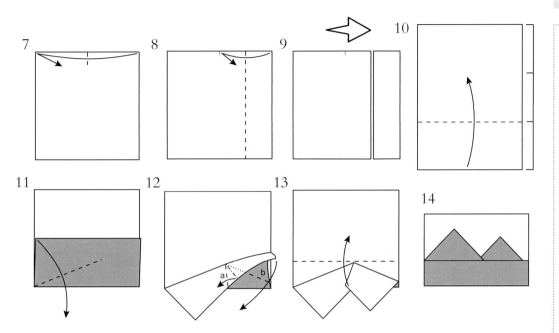

Version 2

You will need a second square of duo or irogami paper and a small pair of scissors. Begin with the side of the paper you wish to form the sky facing toward you.

7 Make a tiny crease to mark the center of the top edge.

8 Fold the right-hand top corner into the center, crease, then unfold.

9 Remove the right-hand quarter of the paper by cutting along the crease made in Step 8. The thinner piece is no longer required. The next picture shows the wider piece on a larger scale.

10 Fold approximately one third of the paper upward. A slight inaccuracy will not matter here.

11 Fold the top left-hand corner of the front flap downward to form the first Pyramid. Be careful only to crease about two-thirds of the way across the paper.

12 Form the second Pyramid by making fold a then fold b. Fold softly at first and only make firm creases once you are sure they will form in the right place.

13 Fold the bottom layers upward using the crease made in Step 10.

14 The result is a much improved version of Egypt. For a perfect picture, both sides of both pyramids should slope at exactly 45°.

intermediate

★★

perfect elephant

Too small to call a herd, we have three different elephants to fold, each with its own origami virtues. Pink Elephant is a hybrid elephant folded from a square. It is hybrid in the sense that while the back half of Pink Elephant is created in the traditional manner by reverse folds, the front half is created in the modern minimalist 'drawing with paper' style. Strip Elephant shows what happens if much the same elephant is folded from a strip of paper rather than a square. The result is a much, much simpler and more elegant design, although the representation of the elephant's tail leaves much to be desired. Three-fold Elephant retains the trunk of Pink Elephant but abandons the color change that separates the trunk from the body as well as any pretence at modeling any kind of tail.

design: david mitchell / paul jackson

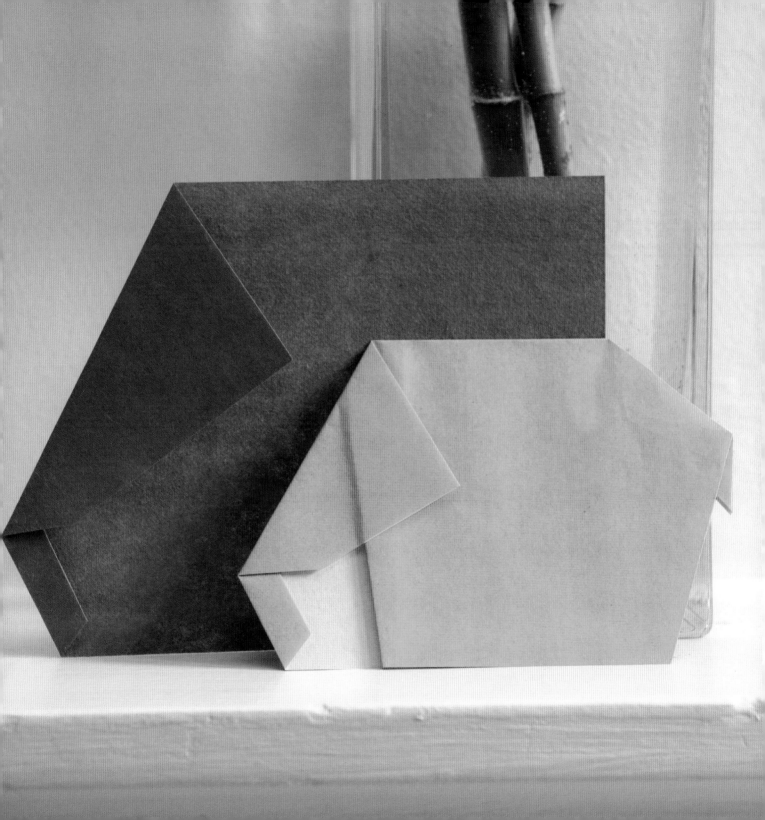

The Perfect Elephant

Perfect Elephant goes against the grain of this book in that it starts with complexity and then moves toward simplicity. It is an attempt to do things the other way around.

   Here we begin with a moderate degree of complexity (well, okay, Pink Elephant is actually very simple in origami terms) and look at how it can be simplified and made more elegant. How can we really make every fold count for something? Presumably by using as few as we possibly can to do the job.

   With the Strip Elephant, the head and trunk were designed by the author, while fellow paperfolder Paul Jackson came up with the idea of using a strip of irogami to create the colour change that separates the head and trunk from the body.

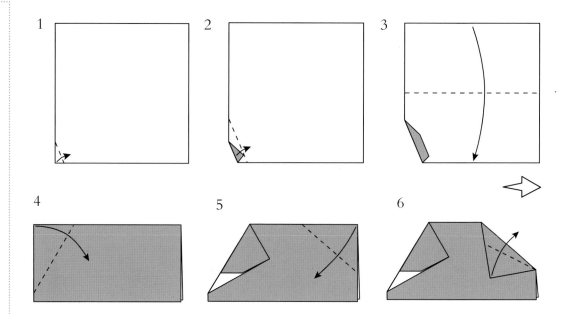

Materials

You will need a square of irogami.

To make Pink Elephant

Begin with the surface you want to form the Elephant's hide facing away from you. It is important to make the folds of this design at the correct angles. The easiest way to do this is to lay your paper on top of the diagrams as you fold.

1 Make a tiny fold in the bottom left-hand corner.

2 Make a second, slightly larger fold at the same angle.

3 Fold the paper in half downward. The next picture is on a larger scale.

4 Fold the top left-hand corner inward as shown. Note that the crease does not go to the bottom corner. Picture 5 shows what the result should look like.

5 Begin to form the tail by folding the top right-hand corner inward.

6 Fold the tip of the tail outward again as shown.

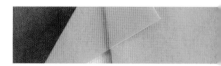

7

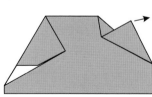

8

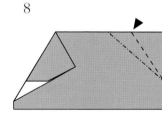

9

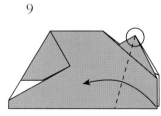

10

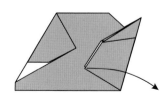

11

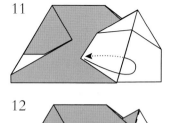

13

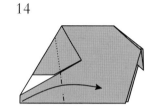

14

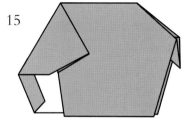

12

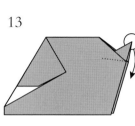

15

7 Open out the folds made in Steps 5 and 6.

8 Pull the layers apart then push the folds gently inside each other to begin to form the tail. Study Step 9 to see what the result should look like.

9 Fold all the layers of the left-hand edge across to the right as shown. Note that the crease bisects the point marked with a circle.

10 Open out the front layer only.

11 Swing this flap in between the other layers by reversing the direction of the existing crease.

12 Fold this flap away in between the other layers in a similar way.

13 Flip the point of the tail inside out and pull it down as far as it will go. Be careful not to tear the paper as you do this.

14 Turn the front layers of the left-hand edge underneath and inside the body to suggest the front legs and reveal the trunk. Look at Step 15 to see what the result should look like.

15 Pink Elephant is finished. A very similar but much simpler elephant can be folded from a long strip.

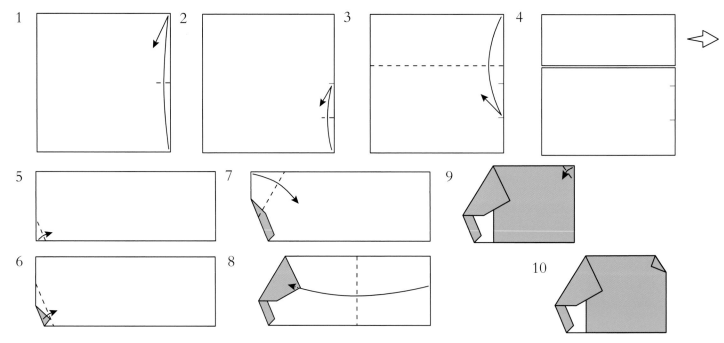

Materials

You will need a square of irogami and a small pair of scissors.

To make Strip Elephant

Begin with the side you want to form the elephant's hide facing toward you.

1 Make a tiny crease to mark the center of the right-hand edge.

2 Make a tiny crease to mark the quarterway point.

3 Fold the top right-hand corner downward onto the quarterway mark, crease, then unfold.

4 Separate the two sections of the paper along the line of the crease made in Step 3. Only the top section is required.

5 Make a tiny fold in the bottom left-hand corner like this.

6 Make a second, slightly larger, fold at the same angle.

7 Form the ears by folding the top left-hand corner inward.

8 Fold the right-hand edge across to the left and tuck it behind the ears, like this.

9 Fold the top right-hand corner inward to form a simple tail.

10 Strip Elephant is finished. An even simpler Elephant can be folded from a shorter rectangle of mono paper by dispensing with the tail and the color change.

1

2

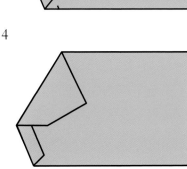

3

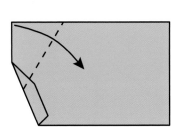

4

Materials

You will need a rectangle of mono paper. Letter paper is the right shape for this elephant, though the result will be better if you use a smaller sheet of the same shape (which you can get by dividing either rectangle into four, eight or 16 equal parts).

To make Three-fold Elephant

1 Make a tiny fold in the bottom left-hand corner.

2 Make a second, slightly larger fold at the same angle.

3 Form the ears by folding the top left-hand corner inwards.

4 Is this the perfect elephant? Probably not. Now that the origami elephant has been reduced close to its bare essentials like this it is clear that all that we need to create a recognizable elephant is the bulk of the body and the suggestion of ears and a trunk.

intermediate
★★

shipwreck

It is possible to combine elements folded from several different sheets of paper to create a single design. This kind of origami, known as multi-piece origami, is particularly popular in Japan where exhibitions of large pictures or dioramas made from many individual folded pieces of paper are quite common.

Shipwreck is an unusual example of the multi-piece genre. It is folded from four separate pieces of paper which are then laid together to create the image of a partly sunken ship. The bows of the ships are made from two pieces, the deckhouse from another, and the last becomes the funnel. Both the funnel and the deckhouse are provided with flaps which act to keep the elements together.

design: david mitchell

60° Folding Geometry

In folding Shipwreck you will use 60° folding geometry for the first time (see Steps 6 through 8). This kind of folding geometry is very common in origami. Shipwreck also introduces you to the use of templates. Sometimes it is easier to locate a fold by using a template rather than by constructing the necessary location points. Since the deck fits into the bow section it makes sense to use the bow section as a template to fold the deck at the angle required.

The funnel of Shipwreck could be folded directly from a square but it is more elegantly folded from a silver triangle. Some paperfolders shy away from using triangles as starting shapes on grounds of purity, but the greater degree of elegance obtained would seem to easily justify the practice in this particular instance.

1

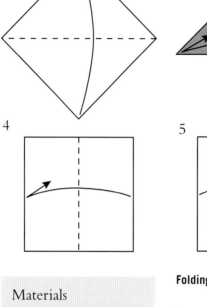

2

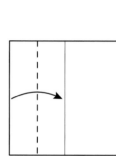

3

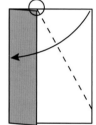

4

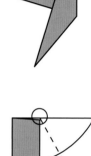

5

6

Materials

You will need three squares of mono, duo or irogami paper and a small pair of scissors. Ideally all the squares should be the same color and size. Only one surface of the paper is visible on the outside of the design.

Folding the Bow

If you are using irogami begin with the paper arranged with the white side facing toward you.

1 Fold the piece in half upward.

2 Fold in half sideways, crease, then open out so that the two halves are at right-angles to each other.

3 The Bow is finished.

Folding the Foredeck

If you are using irogami, begin with the paper arranged with the white side facing toward you.

4 Fold in half sideways, crease, then unfold.

5 Fold the left-hand edge onto the vertical center crease.

6 Fold the right-hand corner onto the left-hand edge making sure the crease starts from the top of the vertical center crease.

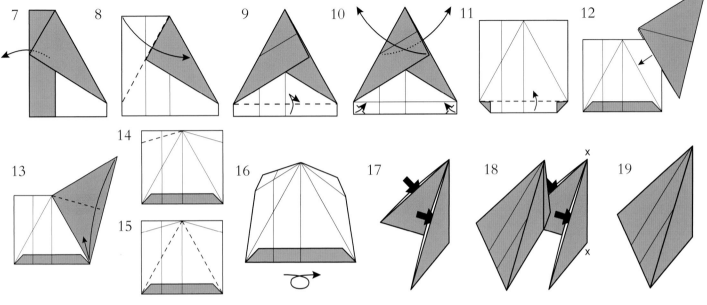

7 Open out the fold made in Step 5.

8 Fold the top left-hand corner onto the sloping right-hand edge so that the top center point becomes sharp.

9 Fold the bottom edge upward using the bottom of the sloping edges as a guide, crease, then unfold.

10 Fold both bottom corners inward as shown, then open out the folds made in Steps 6 and 8.

11 Fold the bottom edge upward using the existing crease.

12 Slide the Foredeck inside the Bow section and align as shown in Step 13.

13 Hold the two pieces firmly in alignment then remake the existing crease in the Bow through all the layers. Crease firmly, then unfold.

14 Remove the Bow then use it to make a second crease on the left-hand half of the paper in a similar way.

15 Lift the top corners up at right-angles using the creases made in Steps 6 and 8.

16 Turn over and fit to the Bow as shown.

17 The flaps of the Foredeck fit into the holes in the Bow.

18 When inserting the flaps of the Foredeck into the holes in the Bow you need to make sure the ends of both flaps slide around edge xx (in opposite directions). This is what holds the assembly together.

19 This is the result. The Bow and Foredeck assembly is finished.

Combining Multiple Sheets

Multi-piece designs are created by arranging several folded elements. Glue is often used to hold the elements in place, especially in large dioramas, but the use of glue is essentially in conflict with the pure origami ethic. A well-designed and presented multi-piece arrangement should stay in place without needing to be glued there.

Representational origami is not only about animals, fish and flowers. It is also about nailclippers, keys, dragons, musical instruments, abstract form and, yes, sunken ships. Unusual subjects pose a challenge to the origami designer because you have to think much more carefully about how to approach them. Modeling an unusual subject often requires coming up with an unusual point of view. It challenges the creativity of the mind as well as the fingers.

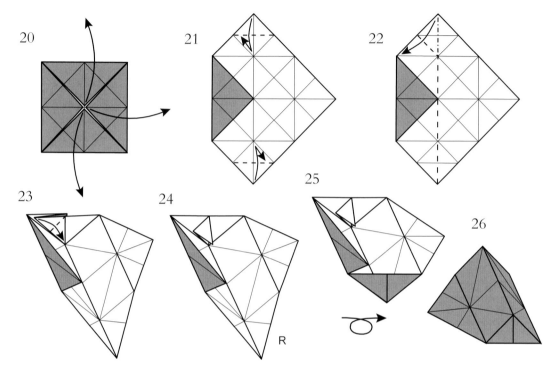

Folding the Deckhouse

Begin with steps 1 through 12 of the Piranha (page 46). If you are using irogami do this without turning the paper over between steps 8 and 9 so that the color is on the outside as shown in picture 20 here.

20 Open out three of the blintzes.

21 Fold the small squares at the top and bottom in half, crease, then unfold.

22 Fold the top corner onto the top point of the front flap. The design will become three-dimensional as you make this fold.

23 Make this tiny fold to lock the layers together.

24 Turn the model around and repeat Steps 22 and 23 on the other end of the paper.

25 Turn the piece over.

26 The Deckhouse is finished.

27

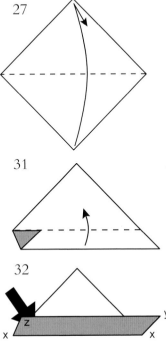

28

29

30

31

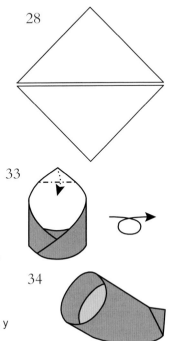

33

32

34

35

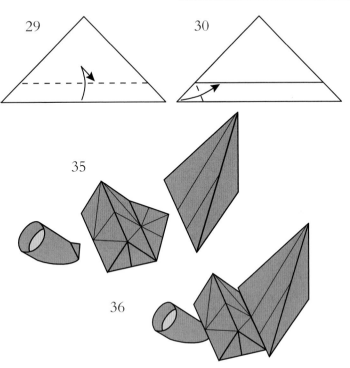

36

Folding the Funnel

If you are using irogami begin with the paper arranged with the white side facing toward you.

27 Fold in half upward, crease, then unfold.

28 Separate the triangles by cutting along the line of the crease. Only one triangle is required.

29 Fold the bottom edge upward in the way shown here, crease, then unfold.

30 Fold the bottom left-hand corner inward so that the result looks like Step 31.

31 Remake Fold 29.

32 Curl xx toward you and insert point y into pocket z to form a ring.

33 Fold the tip of the top point backward at right angles, then turn over.

34 The Funnel is finished.

Arranging the pieces

35 Arrange the three parts of the design like this, then place them together in the way shown in Picture 36 so that the small raised flaps at the front of the Funnel and the Deckhouse hold all three parts together.

36 This is the result. Shipwreck is finished.

intermediate
★★

coasters

The coasters in question here are not shore-hugging ships but the kind of mats you rest your drink on. The original coaster was a wine holder on wheels that could 'coast' around the table, but has evolved to become a static table protector. In origami, however, the word has lost even that connotation and just means a flat, polygonal decoration, usually made by combining two or more pieces of paper.

design: david mitchell

Integrating Multiple Sheets

The term multi-piece origami is reserved for designs where the final result is created by an arrangement of the folded elements. Where they are integrated, i.e. don't fall apart when you pick them up, the technique is called modular origami. Using glue does not count. The individual pieces, or modules, must be designed so that they fit firmly together to form the final shape.

There are degrees of integration. The 1-fold Coaster is more multi-piece than modular. It does hold together, just, thanks to friction. The other Coasters are integrated in a much more solid way.

Modular origami, also known as unit origami, is a huge and rapidly developing field. Many different assembly systems (the way the modules are integrated with each other) are in use.

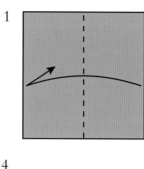

1

2

3

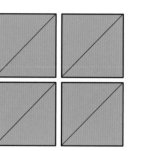

4

5

6

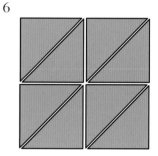

Materials

You will need several squares of duo or irogami paper and a small pair of scissors. Each coaster is folded from four small silver triangles. Eight silver triangles can be obtained from a large square in the way shown in pictures 1 through 6.

Making silver triangles

1 Fold in half sideways, crease, then unfold.

2 Fold in half upwards, crease, then unfold.

3 Separate the small squares by cutting along the creases.

4 Fold each small square in half diagonally, crease, then unfold.

5 Separate the silver triangles by cutting along the creases.

6 You will need four of these silver triangles to make each coaster.

7

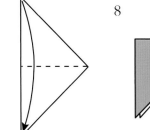

8

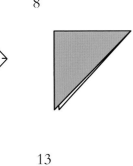

9

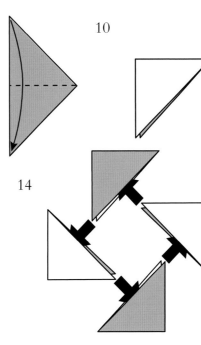

10

11

12

13

14

15

The 1-fold Coaster

Arrange two triangles so that the white surface is facing toward you and two the other way up.

7 Fold in half downward.

8 Make two.

9 Fold in half downward.

10 Make two.

11 You should now have two sets of two modules like this.

12 Two modules fit together like this.

13 Make sure both flaps of the right-hand module go in between the layers of the one on the left.

14 This is how all four modules fit together.

15 When all the modules are pushed fully together the 1-fold Coaster is finished. This is the simplest design in modular origami.

Minimalist Modular Origami

The integration of modules within a design makes it possible to create complex sculptures of great beauty. The final project in this book, Stargate (see page 154), is a good example of what is possible. Coasters are examples of the opposite approach. How simple can an integrated design get? Well, not much simpler than this.

Because these coasters are square, they can be used as tiles and can be laid together to create tiling patterns.

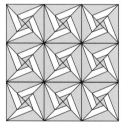

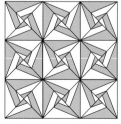

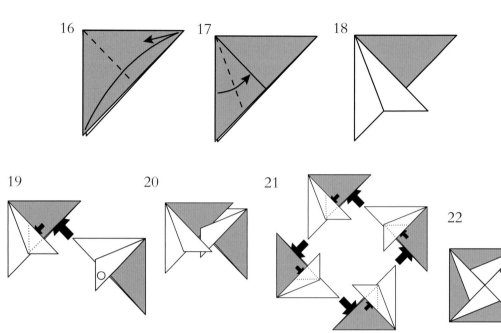

The Rotor Coaster

Begin by arranging all four triangles so that the white surface is facing toward you and folding them in half in the way shown in Step 7.

16 Fold the front layer in half diagonally, crease, then unfold.

17 Fold the left-hand edge of the front layer onto the crease made in Step 16.

18 Make four.

19 Two modules fit together like this. Note that the flap marked with a circle goes underneath the similar flap on the host module.

20 Like this.

21 This is how all four modules fit together.

22 When all the modules are pushed fully together the Rotor Coaster is finished.

The Spiral Coaster

Begin by folding all the triangles to Step 11 of the 1-fold Coaster.

23 Fold the front layer in half diagonally.

24 Fold the front layer in half downward.

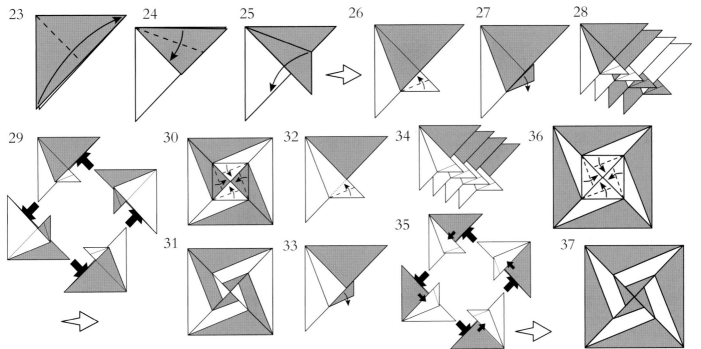

23 24 25 26 27 28

29 30 32 34 36

35

31 33 37

25 Swing the front flaps diagonally downward by opening out the crease made in Step 23.

26 Fold the small triangular flap in half upwards.

27 Undo the fold made in Step 26.

28 Make all four modules. Remember that in two of them the colors will be reversed.

29 The modules go together like this. Note that this time the front flaps go in front of the similar flaps on the host modules.

30 Remake the fold made in Step 26 in each module in turn, working counterclockwise around the design. Tuck the tip of the last flap underneath the first.

31 The Spiral Coaster is finished.

The Double Rotor Coaster

Begin by arranging all the triangles so that the white surface is facing toward you and folding them to Step 18 of the Rotor Coaster.

32 Fold the point of the front flap in half upward.

33 Open out the fold made in Step 32.

34 Make all four.

35 The modules go together like this. Note that the points of the front flaps on the guest modules lie on top of the front flaps on the host modules.

36 Remake the fold made in Step 26 in each module in turn, working counterclockwise around the design. Tuck the tip of the last flap underneath the first.

37 The Double Rotor Coaster is finished.

advanced
★★★

artifact

Artifact is a three-dimensional sculpture made from six silver rectangles, each of which is folded into an identical module. Two modules will fit together to form an open ring. Artifact is made by combining three rings in a Borromean relationship (a mathematical relationship in which none of the three parts are connected to any other part but, despite all this, they can't be taken apart), then by folding in the corners of the rings to lock the assembly together. Once fully assembled the structure is very strong. This famous pattern was the symbol of the Borromeo family in Italy in medieval times, though the design itself is much older than that.

design: david mitchell

Silver Triangles and Rectangles

Silver rectangles are rectangles which have sides in the proportion of 1:root2. This sounds scarily mathematical until you realise that we are just talking about the shape of British A4 paper. The great thing about A4 paper, and any other silver rectangle, is that if you divide it in half along the longer edge, the two smaller rectangles you end up with will be the same shape as the paper you started with. This makes it very easy to scale origami designs folded from this shape of paper.

If you have folded Shipwreck you will already have created a silver triangle. It's the isosceles triangle that you get when you cut a square in half diagonally. It's called a silver triangle because it shares the property that you can fold it in half and end up with two smaller versions of the shape you started with.

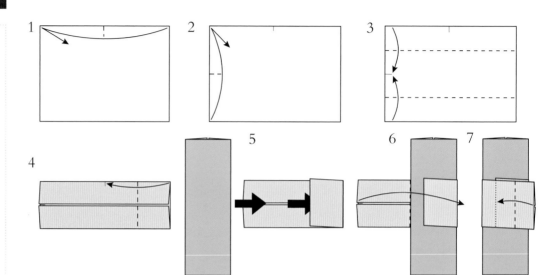

Materials

Materials required: You will need six silver rectangles of mono, duo or irogami paper. Only one surface of the paper is visible on the outside of the finished design.

The diagrams show how to make Artifact from three sets of two modules in each of three colors but the design works equally well in just a single color or using patterned paper. Only one side of the paper is visible in the final design so any kind of paper is equally suitable.

Begin with the paper arranged so that the surface you want to show on the outside of the design is facing toward you.

Folding the module

1 Make a tiny crease in the center of the top edge.

2 Mark the middle of the left-hand edge in a similar way.

3 Fold both the top and bottom edges into the center using the crease made in Step 2 to locate the folds. Fold all six silver rectangles to this stage.

4 Fold the right-hand edge inward using the crease made in Step 1 to locate the fold.

5 Insert a second module underneath the front flap to act as a template.

6 Wrap the right-hand edge of the first module around the template as tightly as possible without damaging either. Crease firmly.

7 Fold the right-hand edge of the front layers across to the right and align it to the left-hand edge of the layer underneath.

8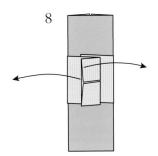

9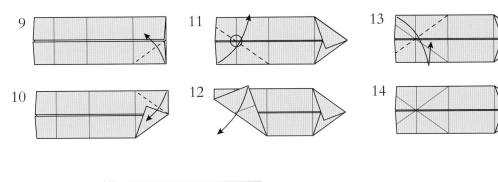

10

11

12

13

14

15

8 Open out the folds made in Steps 4, 6 and 7 and remove the template.

9 Fold the lower right hand section of the module in half diagonally upward.

10 Fold the top right-hand section of the module in half diagonally downward.

11 Fold the lower left-hand section of the module in half diagonally upward, making sure the crease goes through the point marked with a circle.

12 Open out the fold made in Step 11.

13 Repeat Fold 11 on the top left-hand corner in a similar way.

14 Open out the folds made in Steps 9 and 10.

15 Use the existing creases to configure the module into the form shown in Step 16.

16

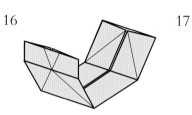

17

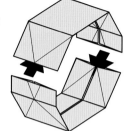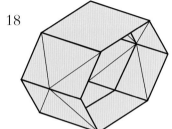

18

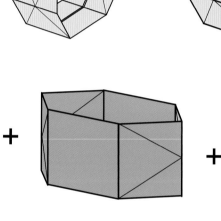

19

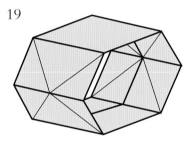 **+** 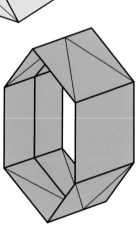 **+**

Assembling Artifact

16 Fold all six modules to this stage.

17 Form two modules of the same colour into a ring by inserting the shorter end flaps inside the longer ones.

18 The result should look like this.

19 Artifact is made by combining three rings in a Borromean relationship, like this:

20

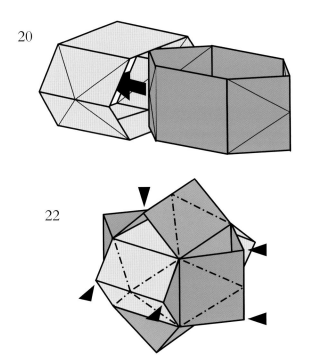

21

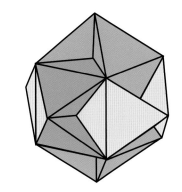

22

23

20 Slide the second ring inside the first.

21 The remaining modules must be added individually through the holes between the first and second rings, then linked together to form the third ring once they are in place.

22 Lock the rings together by turning all the corners inside out using the existing creases.

23 This is the result. Artifact is finished.

advanced

★★★

dresden bowl

The Dresden Bowl is probably the most beautiful bowl in origami. It is a crease and collapse design based on an initial division of the square into a 3x3 grid. If you look carefully at Step 21 of the diagrams, you will also notice that the central square is being collapsed into the form of a water bomb base, which is the foundation for the Chinese Goldfish design. However different they may appear, almost all origami designs depend on a common pool of design ideas. The name Dresden Bowl relates to the reputation of Dresden as a center for the production of fine porcelain and an acknowledgment of the fact that this design was first taught at the Origami Deutschland Convention in Dresden in 2006.

design: david mitchell

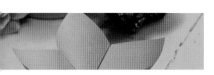

The 3x3 Grid Template

The Egypt design on page 92 required an approximate division of the edge of the paper into three roughly equal parts. Because this division into thirds was only approximate it could be done by eye. To make the Dresden Bowl, however, we need to divide the square accurately into thirds in both directions. There are many ways of doing this, but the best method is to use another square of the same size as a template. This process is explained in Steps 1 to 8 of the diagrams. The result is a starting square divided into a 3x3 grid of nine smaller squares, an extremely useful standard in origami. It also forms the basis of the Enigma Bowl and Gaia projects.

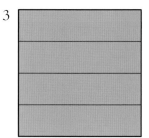

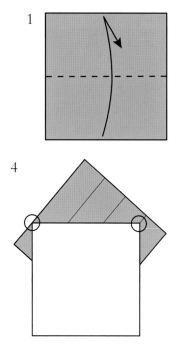

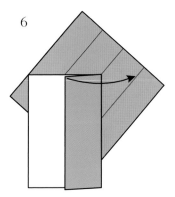

Materials

You will need a single square of mono, duo or irogami paper. Both surfaces of the paper are visible on the outside of the finished design. You will also need a second square of any kind of paper to use as a template to help you fold the first square into a 3x3 grid of smaller squares.

1 Fold the template in half upward, crease, then unfold.

2 Fold both the top and bottom edges to the middle, crease, then unfold.

3 The template is finished.

4 Lay your paper in front of the template like this. Make sure the side you want to form the inside of the bowl is facing toward you.

5 Fold the right-hand corner inward as shown. Make sure the two squares don't slip out of alignment as you make this fold.

6 Open out the fold made in Step 5 and remove the square from the template.

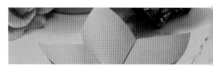

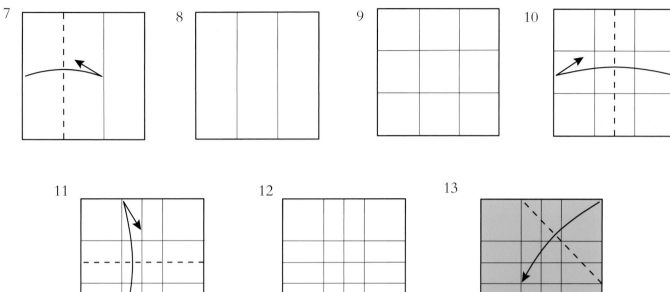

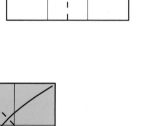

7 Fold the left-hand edge onto the crease made in Step 5, crease, then unfold.

8 Your paper is now divided into thirds. To divide the paper into thirds in the alternate direction as well, rotate through 90° and repeat Steps 4 through 7.

9 This is the result. The paper is now divided into nine smaller squares.

10 Fold in half sideways, crease, then unfold.

11 Fold in half upwards, crease, then unfold.

12 Turn the piece over.

13 Fold the top right hand corner inwards.

Creating Curves

In origami design, curves can be created in two quite separate ways. In the Flying Crane parts of the designs were curved by hand after the folding of the design had been completed. It is also possible to arrange the tension between different parts of the design in such a way that curves are induced within the design during the folding process. This induced curvature is achieved by omitting part of some structural creases. If you look at Steps 16 and 17 of the diagrams you will see that the diagonal creases made in these steps are only made across the central square of the grid. They do not extend to the outside corners. If they did, the outside edges of the bowl would be pointed rather than curved, and the whole design would lose the tension that holds it in shape. This tension comes from the resistance that the paper has to becoming curved.

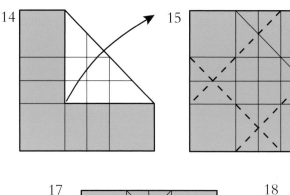

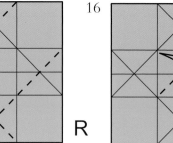

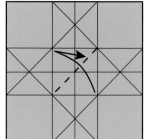

R

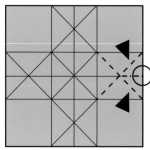

14 Open out the fold made in Step 13.

15 Repeat Folds 13 and 14 on the other three corners.

16 Make a diagonal crease across the central square. Be very careful to make sure the crease does not extend into either of the corner squares

17 Make a second diagonal crease across the central square in the opposite direction. Be very careful to make sure the crease does not extend into either of the corner squares.

18 Pinch the middle of the right-hand edge so that the point marked with a circle rises up toward you.

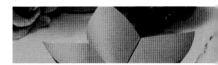

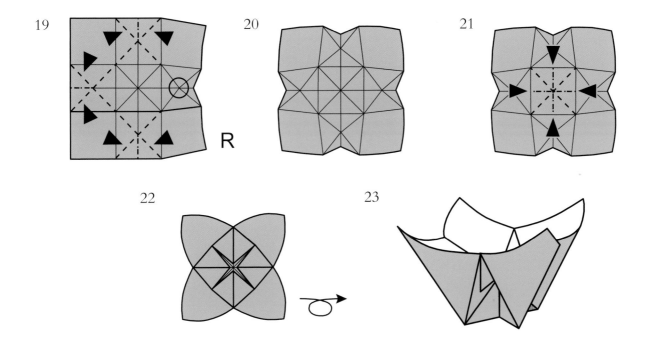

19   The point marked with a circle here should have become concave. Repeat Step 18 on other three sides.

20   This is the result. The central square should be flat but slightly raised. Note that the corner squares are beginning to curve.

21   Pick the paper up, then push all four sides of the central square inward so that the center sinks. As you do this the paper will collapse into the form shown in Step 22.

22   This is the result. Turn over.

23   The Dresden Bowl is finished.

advanced

★★★

lovebird

Lovebird is a design with a secret. It appears just to be a simple irogami sketch of a hovering bird, but it can be held up to the light to reveal a hidden heart. Lovebird was inspired by the British paperfolder Wayne Brown's original Lighthearted design, in which a seemingly uninteresting shape reveals a hidden heart when it is held up to the light. A great design idea, which deserved to be developed further.

design: david mitchell

Using Translucency

Unless it is particularly thick, or dyed a very strong, dark color, most paper is translucent to some degree or other. The possibility of using this translucency as a design feature in origami arises because the degree of translucency of a design diminishes as layers of paper are added. The origami designer can sometimes arrange the layers of the paper within a design to use translucency to good effect. Sometimes this is deliberate, as here in Lovebird, and sometimes an accidental by-product of other design factors. Windfarm, the project on page 148, provides a good example of a design that offers an accidental, but attractive, translucency effect, something that is a common feature of origami tessellations.

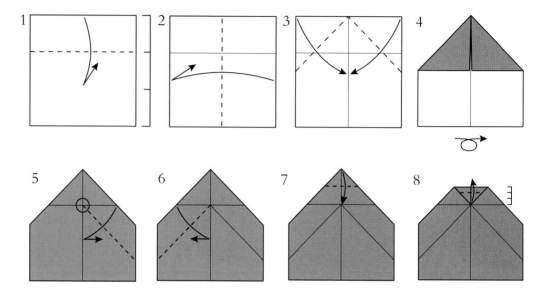

Materials

You will need a square of irogami in a single, strong color that is thin enough to be translucent when held up to the light. Both surfaces of the paper are visible on the outside of the finished design.

Begin with your square arranged so that the white surface is facing toward you.

1 Fold exactly one third of the paper downward, crease, then unfold. A simple way of doing this is shown in Steps 1 through 5 of the Dresden Bowl.

2 Fold in half sideways, crease, then unfold.

3 Fold both top corners into the center.

4 Turn the piece over.

5 Make a diagonal crease in the right-hand half of the paper by folding the horizontal crease onto the vertical one.

6 Make a similar crease in the left-hand half of the paper.

7 Fold the top point downward onto the point where the other creases intersect.

8 Fold approximately two-thirds of the front flap upward again.

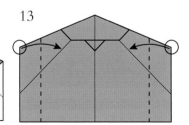

9

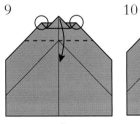

10

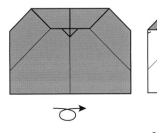

11

12

13

14

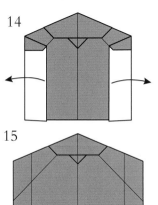

16

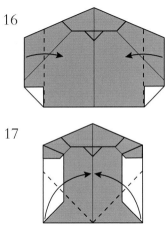

18

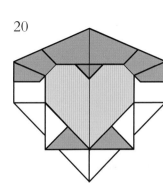

20

15

17

19

9 Fold the top section of the paper downward using the crease made in Step 1.

10 Turn the piece over.

11 Fold each half of the top edge downward onto its corresponding diagonal crease.

12 Turn over. The next picture is on a larger scale.

13 Fold both outside edges inward. Make sure the corners marked with circles end up lying on top of the diagonal creases.

14 Open out the folds made in Step 13.

15 Fold both bottom corners inward using the folds made in Step 13 as guides.

16 Remake the folds made in Step 13.

17 Fold both bottom corners inward.

18 Now fold the bottom corners outward again, taking care to locate the folds in relation to the points marked with circles.

19 Lovebird is finished. When viewed normally only the bird is visible.

20 To see the heart, hold Lovebird in front of a window or lamp.

advanced
★★★

david's star

David's Star is a multi-layer Star of David pre-creased, then collapsed, from a bronze rectangle in two distinct stages. Most origami tessellations collapse flat by the use of a rotational technique known as twist folding. David's Star is a little different. The initial tessellation is three-dimensional rather than flat and is collapsed into shape in just one direction. The tessellation itself then collapses in the opposite direction, which is when some degree of rotation takes place. Sounds complicated? Try it and see. Like many things to do with origami, it is easier to do in practice than it is to explain in words.

design: david mitchell

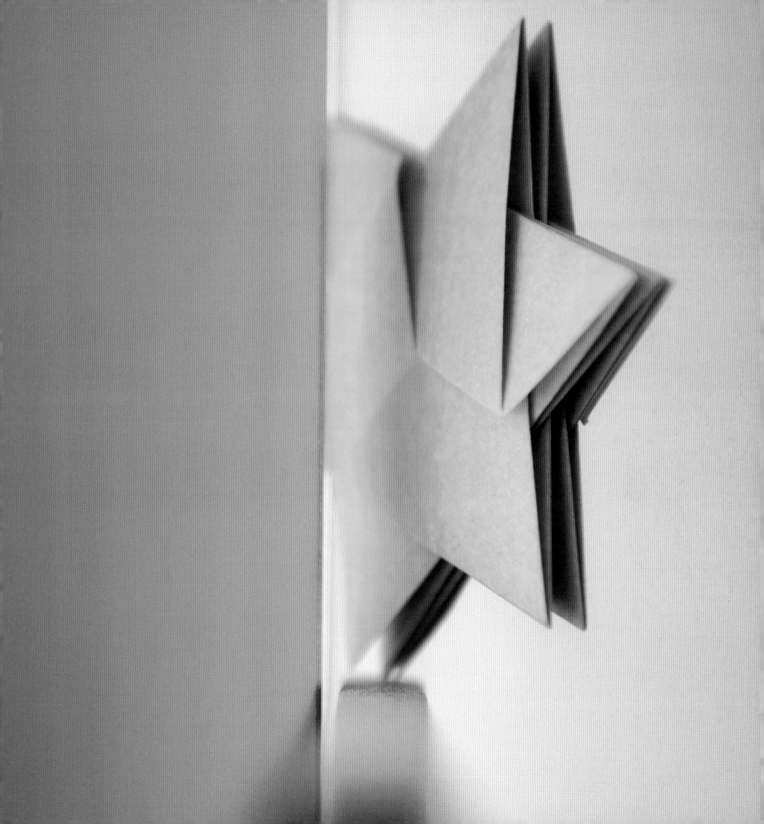

Origami Tessellations

Tessellations are composed of regular shapes which butt up against each other to cover a surface. In origami this kind of design is called a tiling pattern. Origami tessellations are related to tiling patterns but are also entirely different. The difference arises because origami tessellations are folded from a single large sheet of paper. The surface of an origami tessellation may look like a pattern of individual tiles laid edge to edge but it is actually an interconnected matrix of crease and collapse motifs.

Bronze Rectangles

A bronze rectangle is a rectangle with sides in the proportion of 1:root3. It yields a natural 60° folding geometry and so is ideal for using to fold geometric forms. If the bronze rectangle is divided into three equal parts along its longer side, each of the three resulting rectangles will also be bronze.

Materials

You will need two sheets of mono or duo U.S. letter size paper. One sheet is used for the star, the other as a template to help you fold it. Only one surface of the paper is visible on the outside of the finished design. Though there is no equivalent of pre-cut paper available in bronze rectangle proportions, steps 1 to 9 of the diagrams provide an easy method, using a template, for cutting a large bronze rectangle from letter paper.

1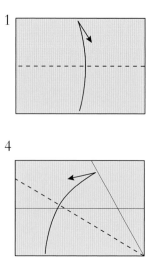

2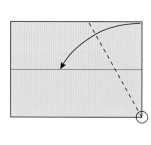

3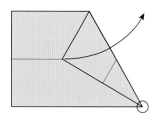

4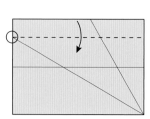

5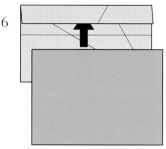

6

Preparing the template

1 Fold in half upward, crease, then unfold.

2 Fold the top right-hand corner onto the horizontal crease, making sure the crease starts from the bottom right-hand corner.

3 Make sure the point of the bottom right-hand corner is sharp. Open out the fold made in Step 2.

4 Fold the bottom edge onto the crease made in Step 2, crease, then unfold.

5 Fold the top edge downward. Use the top left-hand edge of the fold made in Step 4 to locate this new crease accurately.

Making the bronze rectangle

6 Insert the paper you want to fold David's Star from underneath the flap. Make sure you push it all the way in.

7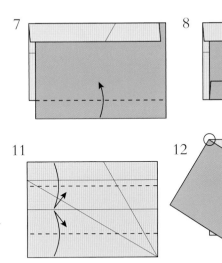

8

9

10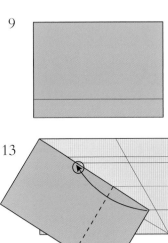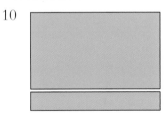

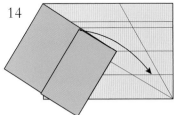

11

12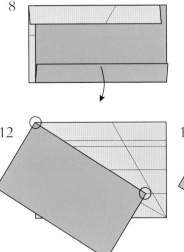

13

14

7 Fold the bottom edge upward along the bottom edge of the template. It is important you do this as accurately as possible.

8 Open out the fold made in Step 8 and remove the paper from the template.

9 Separate the two parts of the paper along the horizontal crease.

10 The larger piece is a bronze rectangle. The smaller piece is no longer required.

Rejigging the template

11 Fold both the top and bottom edges into the center, crease, then unfold.

Folding David's Star

12 Lay the paper on top of the template and align it like this.

13 Fold the top right-hand corner of the paper onto the top edge at the point where it intersects the second to top horizontal crease.

14 Undo the fold made in Step 13.

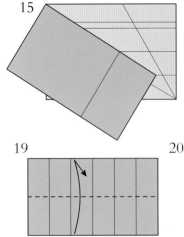

15

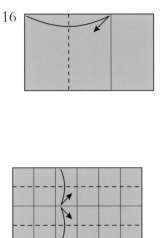

16

17

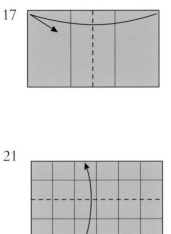

18

22

23

19

20

21

24

15 Remove the paper from the template. The template is not needed any more.

16 Fold the left-hand edge onto the crease made in Step 12, crease, then unfold.

17 Fold in half sideways, crease, then unfold.

18 Fold the two outside thirds in half sideways, crease, then unfold.

19 Fold in half upward, crease, then unfold.

20 Fold the top and bottom edges onto the crease made in Step 19, crease, then unfold.

21 Fold in half upward again.

22 Fold both layers of the top right-hand corner onto the horizontal crease making sure the crease starts from the bottom right-hand corner, crease, then unfold. This is the same type of fold as you made in the template in Steps 2 and 3.

23 The result is a diagonal crease across the right-hand sixth of the paper. Make a similar fold to crease in the other diagonal.

24 Use a similar technique to crease in both diagonals of the third and fifth sixths from the right like this. Try not to make any creases in the other sections as you do this.

25
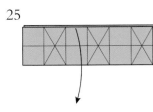

26
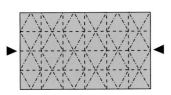

27

28
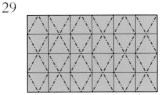

29
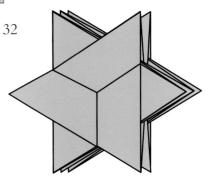

30

31
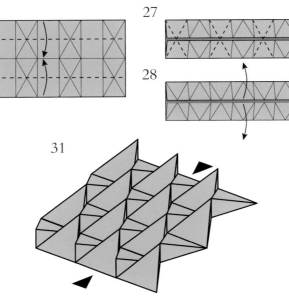

32

25 Open the paper out completely.

26 Fold the top and bottom edges into the middle using the existing creases.

27 Make diagonal creases across the remaining sections of the paper like this.

28 Open the paper out completely.

29 Turn all the diagonal creases into mountain folds. The direction of half of them will need to be reversed to achieve this. Try to do this without putting any new creases in the paper. The crisper your paper remains, the easier the next few steps will be.

30 You now have a grid of creases running in opposite directions through the paper which will allow you to collapse the paper into the three-dimensional tessellation shown in Step 31. Do this slowly starting at one end. Be careful you don't change the direction of any of the creases at this stage. The collapse will not work if you do.

31 Once you have reached this stage it is possible to gently collapse the tessellation sideways into David's Star. Sometimes this collapse just seems to happen by itself. Sometimes the paper needs persuading a little. The more accurately and cleanly you have folded, the less persuasion the paper will need. Persevere, gently. It is possible!

32 If necessary, re-arrange the flaps at the front and back to create a symmetrical appearance. David's Star is finished.

advanced

★★★

enigma bowl

The Enigma Bowl is a complex geometrical paperfold of great intrinsic beauty which can also be put to practical use. The flat rim of the bowl is an eight-pointed star surrounding an octagonal hole, while the base of the bowl is a square. In order to accommodate these differences, the final move stretches the corners into triangular facets creating a three-dimensional effect.

design: david mitchell

Complex Bases

In the earlier projects we saw that traditional origami bases are configurations of folds that act as points of departure from which many origami design journeys can be undertaken. A base can be viewed as a place where the path splits. Complex bases are not difficult to create, but it is difficult to find one which offers as many opportunities for development in as many different ways as the much simpler traditional bases.

My personal favorite is the enigma base. Not only can it be developed in numerous interesting ways — only two of which, the Enigma Bowl and Gaia, are explained in this book — but the folding sequence that creates it is perhaps the most elegant in the whole of origami. Every move creates potential for development which is taken advantage of by the next. In fact this sequence is worth folding over and over just for the sheer pleasure of it, even if you never go on to finish folding the designs themselves.

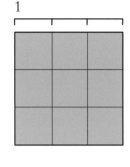

1

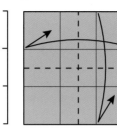

2

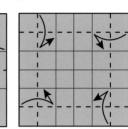

3

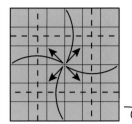

4

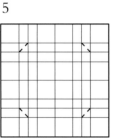

5

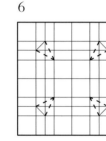

6

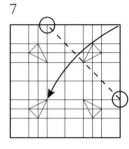

7

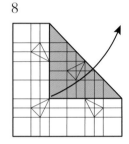

8

Materials

You will need two squares of mono, duo or irogami paper, one to use as a template and one to fold the bowl from. Arrange the square that you want to fold the bowl from so that the surface you want to form the decorative rim of the bowl is facing toward you.

1 Begin by dividing each sheet into a 3x3 grid of smaller squares. Steps 1 through 9 of the Dresden Bowl show you how to use a template to do this.

2 Fold in half edge to edge both ways, crease, then unfold.

3 Fold each of the outside thirds in half, crease, then unfold.

4 Fold each edge into the center in turn, crease, then unfold.

5 Make four tiny diagonal creases in the way shown here.

6 Crease in the other sides of four tiny triangles.

7 Fold the top right-hand corner inward diagonally.

8 Open out the fold made in Step 7.

9
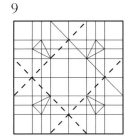

10
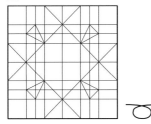

11
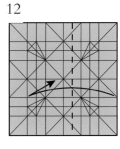

12
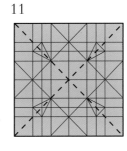

13
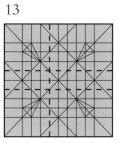

14
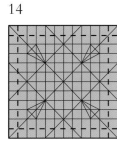

15
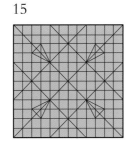

16
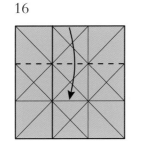

17
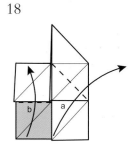

18

9 Repeat Steps 7 and 8 on the other three corners.

10 Turn the piece over.

11 Crease in both diagonals.

12 Fold the right-hand edge onto the vertical crease nearest the left-hand edge, crease, then unfold.

13 Add three further creases in a similar way.

14 Complete the 12x12 grid by folding the outer sixths in half all the way round.

15 Check that you have made all these creases before moving on.

The remaining pictures would be too difficult to read if all these creases were shown all the time. From here onward only the creases you need to see to understand the folding instructions are shown.

16 Fold the top third of the paper downward.

17 Make fold a then fold b using the existing creases.

18 Make fold a then fold b using the existing creases.

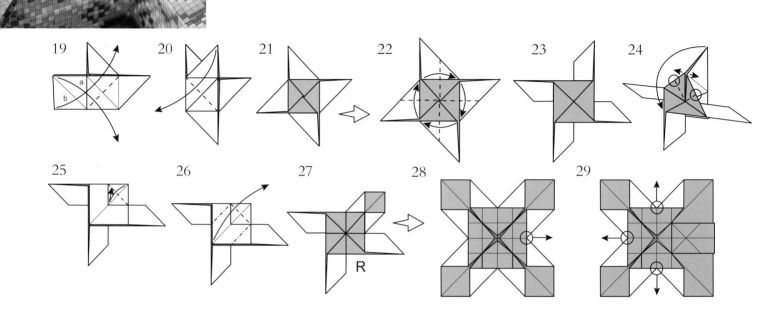

19 Make fold a then fold b using the existing creases.

20 Open out the remaining flap.

21 This form is known as the Pinwheel. The next picture is on a larger scale.

22 Take the right-hand arm of the Pinwheel and fold it in half downward in the way shown. This fold is made through all the layers of the arm. Repeat this fold on the other three arms working counterclockwise around the design. The paper will not lie flat until you have completed all four folds. Flatten and crease firmly.

23 This is the result. Lift one of the arms upward and toward you so that it looks like Step 24.

24 Open the center of this arm then squash it flat. The centers of the two flaps marked with circles fold away from you to allow this to happen. Step 25 shows what the result should look like.

25 Fold the top right-hand corner inward using the existing creases as a guide, crease firmly, then unfold.

26 Fold the front flap up to the right using the crease made in Step 25 and squash symmetrically. The two creases marked with mountain fold lines will form as you flatten the flap into its new position.

27 Repeat steps 24 through 26 on each of the other three arms in turn. The next picture is larger scale.

28 This is the result. Take hold of the front layer at the point marked with a circle and pull gently to the right. Squash symmetrically to look like Step 29. All the creases you need to do this are already there.

29 Repeat Step 28 on each of the other three edges in turn.

30 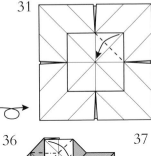 31 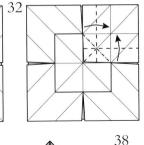 32 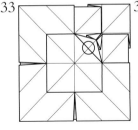 33 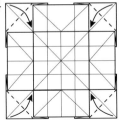 34

35 36 37 38 39 40

30 This is the enigma base. Turn over.

31 Fold the top right-hand corner of the central square inward.

32 Fold the left-hand and bottom edges of the front layers outward simultaneously. The result of this is shown in Step 33.

33 Fully flatten the flap marked with a circle and repeat Folds 31 and 32 on all four corners of the central square.

34 Fold all four corners inwards.

35 Make these two folds simultaneously. As you flatten them, other folds will automatically form behind them. Flatten these as well. You don't need to make any new creases when doing this. Folds that automatically entail making other folds like this are known as swivel folds.

36 The result should look like this. Repeat Fold 35 on the other three corners.

37 Flatten all the creases firmly then turn over.

38 Insert your fingers in the center of the design to open out the body of the bowl along the existing crease lines shown. As you do this, small triangular collars (created by the creases made in Steps 5 and 6) will appear and flatten inside the bowl at each corner. This maneuver is difficult, but persevere, the result is worth it. The position of the collars inside the corners of the bowl can clearly be seen in Step 40.

39 The result is an octagonal hole with a square base. The position of the triangular collars is indicated by the dotted lines.

40 The Enigma Bowl is finished.

advanced
★★★

gaia

Gaia is a complex hexoid (a six-part modular assembly) made from modules developed from the enigma base. The modules are initially configured so that they can be assembled in the form of a stubby star, but the development of the form continues after this assembly is achieved. As the flaps that form the points of the stubby star are opened up, Gaia changes shape and offers further opportunities for development. Opening up the flaps also opens windows in the external surface of the form and allows the light inside, as well as exposing some of the interior surface of the paper to view. Only a very small number of modular forms are capable of further development after the modules have been assembled in this way.

design: david mitchell

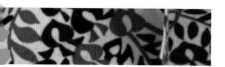

Developing Complex Form

Modular origami offers the designer the potential to create complex sculptural form which goes far beyond what can be achieved from a single uncut sheet. It allows the designer the possibility of opening windows into the form and creating interior as well as exterior surfaces and space.

Some origami modules can be assembled into many different forms. To achieve this the modules must themselves be folded into a slightly altered form, although the basic structure of the module, such as the tabs, pockets and overlapping areas, remain unaltered. These diagrams show how to configure the Gaia modules so that they initially go together to form a stubby star but it is also possible to configure them in a cube form. The same final result can be achieved by opening out the corners in a similar way.

Materials

You will need six squares of mono, duo or irogami paper. Both surfaces of the paper are visible on the outside of the finished design. For the sake of clarity, the diagrams have been drawn to show how to make Gaia from two squares in each of three colors of irogami but in practice the best result is perhaps obtained by using six identical sheets of patterned duo.

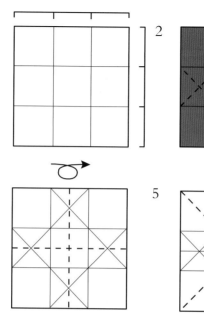

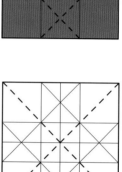

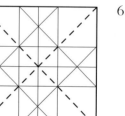

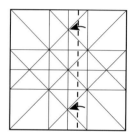

Folding the modules

Begin by following Steps 1 through 8 of the Dresden Bowl to divide your squares into a 3x3 grid (see page 120).

1 Turn over.

2 Make these four diagonal creases (see Steps 13 through 15 of the Dresden Bowl).

3 Turn the piece over.

4 Crease in both bisectors.

5 And both diagonals.

6 Pleat the paper to make the new crease shown here.

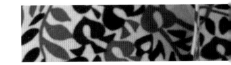

7 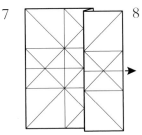   8 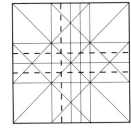   9 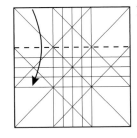   10 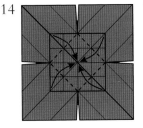   11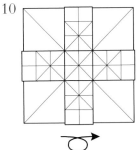

12 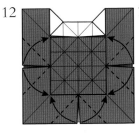   13 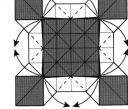   14 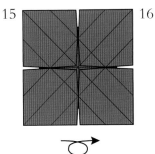   15 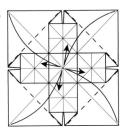   16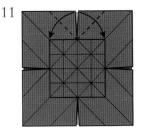

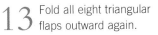

7 Open the pleat out again.

8 Add these three creases in a similar way.

9 Fold the top third of the paper downward. This fold is identical to Step 14 of the Enigma Bowl except that your paper is the other way up so that the relative positions of the white and colored areas are reversed. Continue by following Steps 15 through 27 of the Enigma Bowl until the paper looks like Step 10 here.

10 This is the result. Turn over.

11 Make the two folds shown then flatten the underlying layers so that the result looks like the picture.

12 Repeat Step 11 on the other three edges.

13 Fold all eight triangular flaps outward again.

14 Fold all four corners of the central square into the center. Crease firmly.

15 Turn the piece over.

16 Fold all four corners to the center, crease, then unfold.

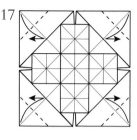

17

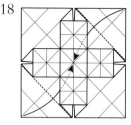

18

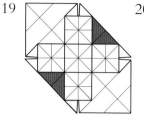

19

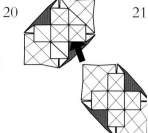

20

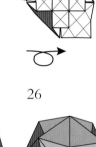

21

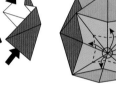

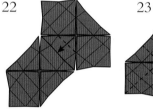

22

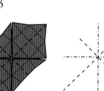

23

24

25

26

17 Fold all four corners inward as shown, crease, then unfold.

18 Fold two opposite corners inward using the creases made in Step 16 but this time tuck them into the pockets underneath the front layers. Make sure the points of the flaps go right into the points of the pockets.

19 The Gaia module is finished. Make six.

Integrating and configuring the modules

20 Two modules go together like this.

21 Turn over.

22 The modules can be locked together by folding back this flap. Now you understand how this works take the modules apart again.

23 Apply this crease pattern to each module and configure it into the form of a Preliminary Fold. Set the creases in by squashing the fold flat both ways, then allow the natural spring in the creases to open out the module into a three-dimensional form.

24 This is a simplified drawing showing what the modules should look like once they have been configured.

Assembling Gaia

25 Using the method explained in Step 20 combine the six modules into the form of a pimpled octahedron.

26 This is the result. Find one of the six stubby points where the valleys between the pimples meet and open up the four triangular flaps at right angles or slightly beyond. As you do this the point will flatten and become the center of a small square face.

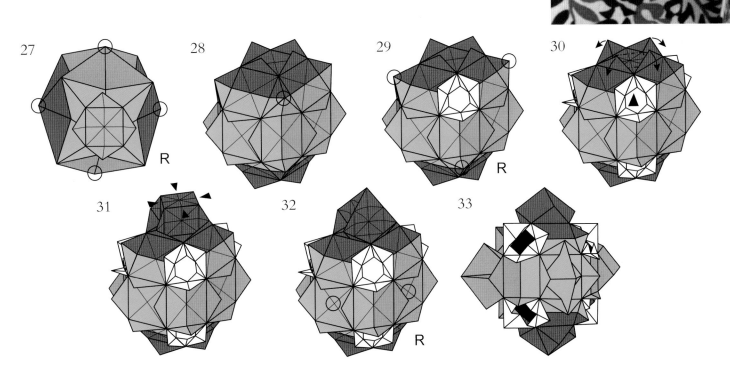

27 Execute Step 31 on the five other similar corners (four of which are marked with circles here). The design will change shape entirely (to a shape based on the mathematical form known as the rhombicuboctahedron) as you do this. This process also serves to lock the modules together.

28 Now open up the three similar flaps which form the corner marked with a circle here.

29 You have opened a window into the interior of the Gaia assembly. There are seven other identical corners to open up. Three of these corners are marked with circles here.

30 Put a finger inside the design and push the top square face gently upward. Spread the flaps surrounding this square outward. As the layers open up, pinch each corner together in turn to create the shape shown in Step 31. If you are experienced in origami this shape will probably already be familiar to you as the base of many attractive boxes.

31 Press the centers of the sides of the top square face together so that the center of the square rises and becomes a point.

32 Repeat Steps 30 and 31 on the five other similar faces, two of which are shown in the diagram marked with circles.

33 Gaia is finished. Arrange the free standing flaps how you will.

To hang Gaia, tie a small bead onto a piece of cotton and use a needle to thread it through the center of one of the points from the inside out.

To make Gaia stand, create a base by inverting one of the points. You can do this by allowing the center of the top square face to sink while following Step 31.

advanced
★★★

windfarm

Windfarm is a flat origami tessellation folded from a
large square that has been partially sub-divided into a
number of smaller squares and half squares by slits.
The result is an intricate square field covered with 16
rotors each of which rotates in the opposite direction to
its neighbor, something that the turbine blades of a real
windfarm are unlikely to do. If this rotor motif seems
familiar to you it is because you have already come
across it in folding the Rotor and Double Rotor Coasters.

design: david mitchell

Sub-dividing Sheets

The little-used technique of sub-dividing large sheets into smaller ones by using slits is a halfway house between origami tessellations, in which the integrity of the large sheet remains intact, and modular origami, where the small sheets are entirely separate from one another. Here, the smaller sheets of paper remain attached to each other, so retaining the quality of the finished design as a coherent whole, while allowing the smaller sheets to be folded largely independently.

The picture below illustrates how this sub-division into smaller sheets works.

If the slits were made parallel to the edges of the larger sheet, half squares would not occur.

Materials

You will need a single large square of mono, duo or irogami paper. Only one surface of the paper is visible on the outside of the finished design.

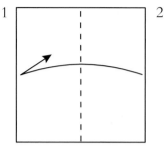

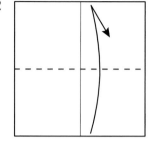

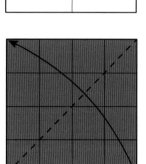

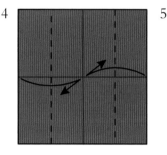

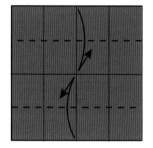

Windfarm is a tessellation of rotor motifs. You need to begin by practicing making a single motif.

Folding practice

You will need a small square of paper of any kind. If you are using irogami begin with the white side up.

1 Fold in half sideways, crease, then unfold.

2 Fold in half upward, crease, then unfold.

3 Turn the piece over.

4 Fold both outside edges into the center crease, then unfold.

5 Fold the top and bottom edges into the center, crease, then unfold.

6 Fold the piece in half diagonally.

7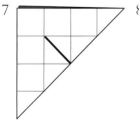

8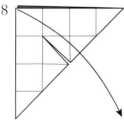

9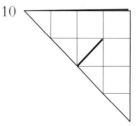

10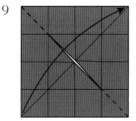

11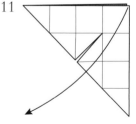

12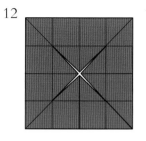

13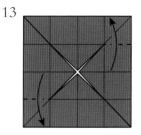

14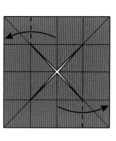

15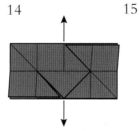

16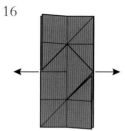

7 Make a cut through both layers in the position marked by the thick black line.

8 Open out the fold made in Step 6.

9 Fold in half diagonally in the alternate direction.

10 Make a cut through both layers in the position marked by the thick black line.

11 Open out the fold made in Step 9.

12 You should now have an X-shaped slit in the center of the paper.

13 Make these two folds simultaneously. The result should look like Step 14.

14 Flatten, then pull out as shown to undo these folds.

15 Make these two folds simultaneously in exactly the same way. The result should look like Step 16.

16 Flatten, then pull out as shown to undo these folds as well.

The Senzaburu Orikata

This technique of sub-dividing large sheets into smaller sheets by means of slits is first found in one of the earliest origami publications, *The Senzaburu Orikata*, published in Japan in 1797. The most complex design featured in the book is the Hundred Cranes. Strangely, perhaps, instructions for creating the Hundred Cranes are not included in the book, and it is not clear precisely how it could be done. In the book, the pattern of slits illustrated would produce almost the correct number of cranes (in fact 97 rather than 100) but the crane folded from a large central square would be much smaller in comparison to the others.

17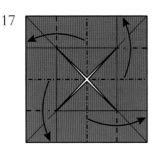

18 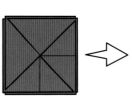 19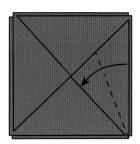

20 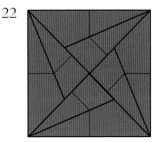 21 22

17 Now make all four folds simultaneously. The result should look like Step 18.

18 This is the result. The next picture is on a larger scale.

19 Fold one of the top flaps in half inward like this.

20 Repeat this fold on the other three top flaps working counterclockwise around the design.

21 Tuck the flap marked with a circle into the pocket behind it.

22 This is the result. This rotor pattern is a classic motif of origami design. Practice is over.

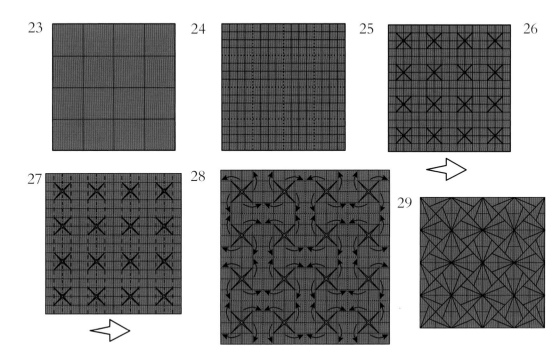

23

24

25

26

27

28

29

30

Folding Windfarm

Windfarm tessellations can be made in many sizes. These diagrams show you how to make a tessellation of 16 rotors from a square. You will need a large square of thin-but-strong paper to do this.

23 Begin by dividing the square into a 4x4 grid.

24 Sub-divide each of the smaller squares into a 4x4 grid as well.

25 Cut the X slits as shown here. Try to crease the paper as little as possible as you do this.

26 Assign all these horizontal creases as either mountain folds or valley folds as shown.

27 Assign all these vertical creases as either mountain folds or valley folds as shown.

28 This diagram shows the direction of rotation of the folds in each cell. Note

that the flaps in adjacent cells rotate in opposite directions. The direction of rotation does not affect the assignment of the creases as mountains or valleys, although not all the valley folds are used. In theory all these folds should be made simultaneously. In practice it is best to start the collapse from one corner and work outward. Each of the rotors can then be formed from the cluster of four flaps within a cell in the way shown in Steps 17 through 20, which you have already practiced.

29 The result should look like this. Windfarm is finished.

30 A different pattern is apparent if Windfarm is held up to the light.

advanced

★★★

stargate

Stargate is a macro-modular sculpture made from five Artifact assemblies linked by joining pieces. Like the Artifact modules, these joining pieces are also folded from silver rectangles. The pentagonal geometry of the finished Stargate sculpture is very attractive, and the finished design also has a secret: a five-pointed star, concealed in the center underneath the outer ring of joining pieces.

design: david mitchell

Integrating Modular Assemblies

One of the difficulties in creating complex modular sculptures using origami is that such designs tend to deform under their own weight. One way around this is to assemble complex forms in stages by combining complete modular assemblies into integrated second-generation structures. This technique is called macro-modular origami.

Modular origami is sometimes defined in terms that suggest all the modules used should be identical. This is often the case, but not a defining characteristic. The key concept in defining modular origami is that of integration. Many excellent designs exist in which several different types of module are integrated within the same structure. The use of joining pieces here is just one example of the opportunities for artistic creativity that the macro-modular approach offers.

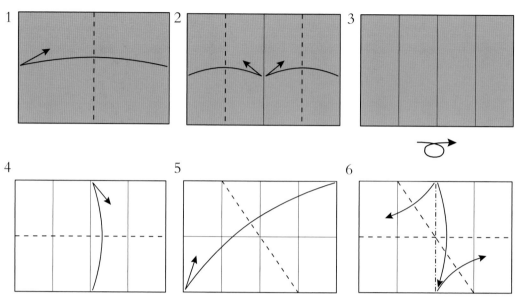

Materials

Stargate is a macro-modular sculpture made from Artifact assemblies linked together with joining pieces. You will need five complete Artifact assemblies and fifteen silver rectangles of mono, duo or irogami to fold the joining pieces from. Only one surface of the paper is visible on the outside of the finished joining pieces.

Folding the joining pieces

Begin with the side of the paper you want to form the visible surface of the module facing toward you.

1 Fold in half sideways, crease, then unfold.

2 Fold both outside edges into the center, crease, then unfold.

3 Turn the piece over.

4 Fold in half upward, crease, then unfold.

5 Fold in half corner to corner, diagonally, crease, then unfold.

6 Remake these folds simultaneously to collapse the paper into the form shown in Step 7.

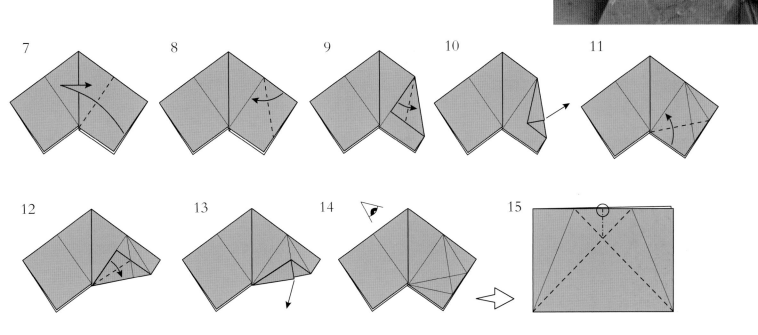

7   This is the result. Remake the sloping right-hand crease through all the layers as shown.

8   Fold the top edge of the right-hand point onto the crease you have just remade in Step 8.

9   Fold the front flap in half to the right.

10   Open out the folds made in Steps 8 and 9.

11   Repeat Step 8 on the bottom edge.

12   Repeat Step 9 on the front flap.

13   Open out the folds made in Steps 11 and 12.

14   The next diagram shows just the right-hand flap, on a larger scale, and drawn from the viewpoint indicated.

15   Remake the two diagonal folds so that the point marked with a circle rises up toward you in the way shown in Step 16.

16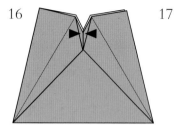

17

18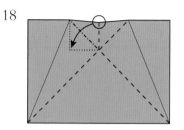

19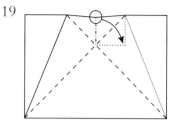

20

21 R

22

23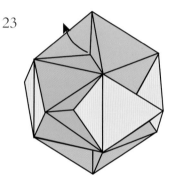

16 Pinch in a new crease then flatten gently.

17 Separate the layers and reverse the direction of these two short creases in the top layer only. The next move is difficult. It cannot be drawn in a single picture. Step 18 shows the fold that is made in the top layer. Step 19 shows the fold that is made in the rear layer. These folds must be made at the same time. Take care you understand what you need to do before you do it and make sure your paper stays crisp.

18 Remake Fold 16 but making sure that the point marked by a circle moves away from you and swings round behind to the left between the layers. The dotted line shows where the flap ends up.

19 Remake Fold 16 but making sure that the point marked by a circle moves toward you and swings to the right between the layers. The dotted line shows where the flap ends up.

20 This is the result. The flap in the top layer has swung behind to the left. The flap in the rear layer has swung in front to the right. Both flaps now lie in between the layers. Fold both outer flaps backward and crease firmly to lock the whole caboodle in place.

21 Your module should now look like this. Turn over sideways and repeat Steps 15 through 20 on the other end of the module. The result should look like Step 22.

22 The Stargate joining piece module is finished. Make all 15.

Attaching the joining pieces

23 Open out one of the sunken corners of the Artifact assembly.

24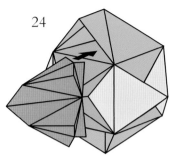

25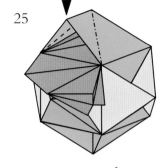

26

27

28

29

30

R

24 Insert one end of the joining module inside the Artifact assembly.

25 Turn the open corner inside out to lock the module in place.

26 The joining piece is now firmly linked to the Artifact assembly.

Assembling Stargate

27 Join the five Artifact assemblies into a ring using five joining pieces like this.

28 Add five more joining pieces in the positions shown here.

29 Turn over and repeat Step 28 on the other side of the design.

30 Stargate is finished. Stargate makes an effective hanging ornament. To hang it, simply open up one of the outside sunken corners and thread a knotted cotton thread up through the center of the corner to the outside.

Resources

Despite the best efforts of the author to make this book as complete as possible it is not feasible to cover every aspect of a subject as large and diverse as origami in this single volume. I have provided a basic introduction to the main techniques and styles so that, if you have read this book from the start to here, and faithfully folded your way through all the designs, you will have a good understanding of what origami is about, its main themes and the ideas that inform good origami design.

If you are hooked and want to learn more, the best way is to contact and talk to other paperfolders since they are a remarkably varied and interesting bunch of people. One easy way to get in contact with other paperfolders and find out more about origami is to join the origami internet mailing list at http://lists.digitalorigami.com/mailman/listinfo/origami. This is by far the best origami list on the internet but even so, remember to take people's opinions with a pinch of salt. Not everyone who posts to the list will know as much as you already do. Some people, though, will know a great deal more.

For further information on Chinese origami tradition and Yuen Bao, mentioned on page 66, read *Chinese Origami* by David Mitchell, Barnes and Noble, ISBN 0-7607-8261-X.

For further information on designing custom bases, mentioned on page 78, see *Origami Design Secrets* by Robert Lang, A K Peters Ltd, ISBN 1-56881-194-2